Trump in the White House

TRUMP
in the White House
TRAGEDY AND FARCE

John Bellamy Foster

Dev Publishers & Distributors
New Delhi

Published by
Dev Publishers & Distributors
Second Floor, Prakashdeep,
22, Delhi Medical Association Road,
Darya Ganj, New Delhi - 110 002

www.devbooks.co.in

ISBN 978-93-81406-78-6

Dev Publishers & Distributors, 2018

Reprinted by arrangement with Monthly Review Press, New York
for sale in South Asia only.

Printed in India.

Contents

Foreword by Robert W. McChesney — 7

Preface — 15

1. Neo-Fascism in the White House — 19

2. This Is Not Populism — 57

3. Trump and Climate Catastrophe — 89

The Nature of Resistance: A Brief Conclusion — 111

Notes — 120

Index — 152

To Carrie Ann

Foreword

by Robert W. McChesney

IN *TRUMP IN THE WHITE HOUSE: Tragedy and Farce*, John Bellamy Foster connects the great and pressing issues of our times, the resolution of which will go a long way toward determining the course of human civilization for generations. Those issues are climate change, capitalist stagnation, and, centrally, the return of fascism to the United States and the global political scene.

When Foster and I were young men—we attended college together in the early 1970s—the term *fascism* was bandied about periodically. It was often used in a pejorative sense, as the ultimate put-down for someone opposed to progressive politics, or just to castigate any unpleasant person on a "power trip." Yet in the United States and Western Europe, the idea that fascism was a plausible political development seemed entirely farfetched. Where it continued to exist, in Franco's Spain for example, its days were numbered. The experience of the Second World War guaranteed that no credible political party or figure would ever advocate such a reprehensible and repudiated political order. By the 1970s, we were all "democrats," at least rhetorically.

When neoliberalism emerged as the dominant political movement in the United States and much of the world by the 1980s, it was careful to distinguish its embrace of so-called free markets and hostility toward trade unions and the welfare state, not to mention socialism, as having nothing to do with fascism or the xenophobia that invariably accompanies fascism. Neoliberals were for a puny and enfeebled government that would not interfere with individuals as they went about their lives however they best saw fit. Government was liberal, the polar opposite of fascist.

The recent emergence of neo-fascist movements in Europe, and now Donald Trump's 2017 ascension to the U.S. presidency, courtesy of the Electoral College, has forced a serious reconsideration of fascism and its relationship to capitalism and to democracy. As Foster notes, in the 1950s Paul Sweezy characterized fascism as the antonym of liberal democracy. And now, with economic stagnation prevalent and seemingly permanent for capitalism worldwide, crises of poverty, inequality, and grotesque political corruption are increasingly the order of the day. Liberal democracy is failing, as social problems are spiraling out of control. Zombie fascism is on the march again.

We are fortunate to have a scholar like Foster tackle this subject. As a leading political economist and theorist, Foster contextualizes fascism and provides an accessible and coherent, yet sophisticated, analysis. And as perhaps the leading environmental sociologist in the world today, Foster connects the emergence of neo-fascism to the climate crisis that threatens the survival of our species. Needless to say, it is a frightening picture at every level.

If one thing becomes clear in reading these essays, it is that the notion that neoliberalism, or "libertarianism," as its boosters prefer to call it, is the polar opposite of fascism is entirely bogus. Libertarianism is, in fact, the other side of the exact same coin. Nancy MacLean provides crucial evidence to this end in her recent book *Democracy in Chains* (Viking, 2017), which details the origins and rise of libertarianism and the radical right in the United States since the 1950s. It is impossible to read the internal correspondence of the masterminds of libertarianism and not see the fundamental contempt for liberal values and the rule of law. Their concern with civil liberties is opportunistic. Shout from the mountaintops about the rights of man when it advances the position of the hard right; remain mute if not be outwardly supportive when leftists are purged.

What becomes clear in MacLean's account is that the masterminds of libertarianism are driven by a contempt for democracy above all else. Their great fear is that anything close to genuine majority rule would be antithetical to the maintenance of existing capitalism, with its extreme wealth inequality, which libertarianism heartily approves. In fact, libertarians, or "free market conservatives," see their most important mission as protecting and extending the class domination of the wealthy few by any means necessary.

This explains the obsession among libertarians (read "neoliberals") to limit the ability of the dispossessed to enjoy the right to vote, to encourage gerrymandering, to allow moneyed interests unchecked power over government officials and bodies, and to do whatever is possible to corrupt effective popular governance and thereby guarantee the rule of capital. But it goes far beyond that. The libertarian obsession has been far more strategic, and its proponents are playing the long game.

On the one hand, the neoliberal movement has been obsessed with conquering the court system and changing the Constitution—or changing interpretations of the existing Constitution, which is effectively the same thing—to reduce the possibility of effective majority rule. The idea is to make it so that no matter who gets elected, the rule of wealth cannot be meaningfully altered or undermined. Just lock in structures that repel the ability of the majority to change course.

On the other hand, the neoliberal/libertarian crowd has been obsessed with eliminating those institutions that make effective political participation in a democracy possible, what is termed the "democratic infrastructure."

What do I mean by this? If you eliminate labor unions and other organizations for those without property, sharply reduce quality public education and a credible independent news media, undermine the independence of public universities, devote billions to generating slick propaganda, make it virtually impossible to launch effective new political parties, and privatize as much of traditional government functions as possible, then having the right to vote is largely handcuffed and ineffectual. You get a "democracy" where the outcome is all but predetermined. The logical result is that people become disenchanted and apathetic, and turn away from politics, dismissing it all as a massive pile of bullshit. And that is precisely the libertarian goal. People should put all their energy into their commercial affairs and leave governance, such that it is, to their economic betters, those who own the society's commanding heights.

In this sense, neoliberalism *is* distinct from fascism; in the former people tune out politics, whereas in the latter people get worked up in a lather over various racist and nationalist "solutions" to the immense problems of a society in crisis and without a functioning governing system.

The neoliberal assault on the "democratic infrastructure" of the United States has been proceeding for a good four decades now and has been significantly completed. It means that the United States is now a formal constitutional republic, but very far from being even a marginally democratic society. And this means that the civil liberties Americans have taken for granted stand on a much flimsier foundation.

This is the central point I am making: what neoliberalism and libertarianism have accomplished in stealth fashion is exactly the outcome that fascist movements invariably seek—a demolished democratic system in which the remaining institutions are controlled by and serve capital or are enfeebled. Our increasingly privatized education system and disintegrating journalism are ideal for propagandists and frauds. It is difficult to see how a preposterous figure like Trump could exist in public life if there were a credible information system.

But wait, the acolytes of Milton Friedman protest, we are principled. We believe in civil liberties and freedom. We hate the surveillance state and some of us even oppose all these wars the United States is constantly fighting. The rhetoric is impressive, and there may be a few rank-and-file libertarians who actually practice what they preach. But history shows that whenever there is a crisis of the system that threatens existing property relations, the libertarians throw in unconditionally with the militarists, madmen, and fascists who tear up any pretense of liberal democracy and engage in wholesale human rights violations and violence against dissidents. The active and enthusiastic participation of University of Chicago economists with the fascist Pinochet dictatorship in Chile in the 1970s is exhibit A in this regard. And in the United States, it is chilling to read in MacLean's book just how quickly the "small government" crowd approved of illegal police violence against protesters in the 1960s.

The neoliberals also protest that they are not racists like the neo-fascists and their policies are motivated by a deep concern for improving the situation of society's least fortunate, regardless of their race or ethnicity. But in MacLean's account, it is even more chilling to read of their disregard, and at times contempt, for the effects of racism in our society. This should be no great surprise as the modern "free market" movement was birthed in close collaboration with vile white supremacists seeking to preserve Jim Crow in the postwar South. The actual history of racial exploitation is incompatible with the neoliberal view of the history and legitimacy of capitalism in the United States, so it gets thrown under the bus.

The libertarian movement, bankrolled significantly by the infamous Koch brothers, has effectively taken over the Republican Party. This has encouraged the neoliberal restructuring of the United States over the past four decades and has paved the way for a figure like Trump, and an incipient neo-fascist administration, to gain power. And the manner in which the Republican Party in Congress has embraced Trump with little hesitation since his inauguration demonstrates that there is considerable common ground in their political economic objectives. If the Republicans do part with Trump it will not be over principles or policies. It will be because Trump will be seen as a bad bet whose bizarre behavior could jeopardize their political fortunes. By any independent account, Trump is a lazy, ignorant, unreflective, and unprincipled sociopath, a blowhard and a dangerous moron—a person who lies so routinely it appears he is incapable of even understanding the idea of truth or falsity. Even the Koch brothers realize this could be a problem to achieving their ambitions.

But Trump's personality is also the basis for his support. It has made him the most powerful person in the world. His unpredictability and the frightening neo-fascist inclinations he encourages are now all of our problems.

The last great wave of global fascism occurred in the 1930s, during the Great Depression. With fascism's inexorable attraction to war and militarism, it led to the Second World War and, with the emergence of nuclear weapons, to the credible concern that it could lead to the extinction of our species. Fortunately, fascism was defeated then, but it would always lurk in the background ready to pounce as long as capitalism exists.

The good news for humanity is that there is nothing inexorable about the victory of fascism. There is another road out, and that road is socialism. Not the single-party dictatorship with its maximum leader that masked its crimes behind the noble term and tradition. But the real thing. A democratic society with real self-government, of the people, by the people, and for the people. An economy that serves the people rather than an economy that demands the people serve the needs of the owners.

That may have sounded like a pipe dream in the past, but it is becoming clear that it is the only credible way out of our present morass. The good news is that people around the world are moving in that direction. It is striking that young people, in particular, are increasingly seeking progressive and humane solutions to the problems before us and have shown little taste for fascism compared to older generations. The numbers are on our side. But the neoliberals and the fascists have always known that, and they hold the reins of power. In this timely book, John Bellamy Foster explains the nature of their project and its implications better than anyone.

Preface

RUNNING FOR PRESIDENT in the Republican primaries in January 2016, Donald Trump half-jokingly told a receptive audience at Dordt College in Sioux Center, Iowa (an institution affiliated with the Christian Reformed Church in North America): "I could stand in the middle of Fifth Avenue and shoot somebody, and I wouldn't lose any voters, OK?" Shaping his fingers like a gun and acting as if he were pulling the trigger, he added, "It's like, incredible."[1] It is this sense of his capacity to act with complete impunity that best defines Trump, the celebrity billionaire, now president of the United States.[2]

The present book, however, is less about the character of the new occupant of the White House, than the rise of the radical right that his election represented, and its historical basis and significance. Although Trumpism is commonly characterized as a form of right-wing populism, the analysis in the following pages focuses on the concrete, sociological reasons for seeing this new political development as a type of neo-fascism, part of the larger fascist genus. Similar political developments are evident in Europe—in the National Front in France, the Northern League in Italy, the Party for Freedom in the Netherlands, the UK Independence Party, the Sweden Democrats, and in similar parties in other countries. In the United States, however, this has taken an even more dangerous form, bringing together white supremacists, Christian fundamentalists, neo-fascists, and capitalist billionaires. This is a tragedy. It is also a farce. It represents "the destruction of reason," best represented by the Trump administration's "ecocidal capitalist" claim that climate change science is a hoax.[3]

The chapters that make up this book were written over the period from Trump's electoral victory in November 2016 up through the final days of April 2017, which ended his first hundred days in office. Although there has been some slight updating to account for major events since that time, the book is meant to cover this unique period in the history of the U.S. presidency, roughly the first six months since the 2016 elections. Understanding the challenges raised by the rise of Trumpism is crucial in recognizing the strategic context of the present. What is needed is active, not passive, resistance by the vast majority of people, the wretched of the earth, aimed at the reconstitution of society as a whole. The alternative is darkness.

I would like to thank Martin Paddio and Michael Yates for inspiring me to make my initial writings on Trump into a book and for their help at various stages in the process. John Mage, as always, gave me sound advice, criticism, and support, without which I could scarcely have gone forward. I am also enormously indebted to others at *Monthly Review*, including Brett Clark, Hannah Holleman, Fred Magdoff, R. Jamil Jonna, Intan Suwandi, Colin Vanderburg, and Victor Wallis, all of whom helped with the copyediting and proofing of the original pieces and provided valuable advice. Erin Clermont copyedited the final book. Robert McChesney kindly agreed to write the foreword. Joseph Fracchia provided his wisdom and sense of history in discussions on the history of fascism. István Mészáros gave me constant encouragement and allowed me to read some of the chapters of his magnificent, though still unfinished, work on the critique of the state. I'm particularly grateful to Naomi Klein for sending me in the first week of June an advance copy of her own book on Trump, *No Is Not Enough: Resisting Trump's Shock Politics*. This was useful in helping me to develop some of the points in this preface. As before, I would like to indicate my deep appreciation to Carrie Ann Naumoff, with whom I discussed all of this, albeit haphazardly, from beginning to end, and whose presence is indelibly marked in these pages.

—June 11, 2017
Eugene, Oregon

Neo-Fascism in the White House

> There is a shadow of something colossal and menacing that even now is beginning to fall across the land. Call it the shadow of an oligarchy, if you will; it is the nearest I dare approximate it. What its nature may be I refuse to imagine. But what I wanted to say was this: You are in a perilous position.
>
> —JACK LONDON, *THE IRON HEEL*[1]

Not only a new administration, but a new ideology has now taken up residence at the White House: neo-fascism. It resembles in certain ways the classical fascism of Italy and Germany in the 1920s and '30s, but with historically distinct features specific to the political economy and culture of the United States in the opening decades of the twenty-first century. This neo-fascism characterizes the president and his closest advisers, and some of the key figures in his cabinet.[2] From a broader sociological perspective, it reflects the electoral bases, class constituencies and alignments, and racist, xenophobic nationalism that brought Donald Trump into office. Neo-fascist discourse and political practice are now evident every day in virulent attacks on the racially oppressed, immigrants, women, LBGTQ people, environmentalists, and workers. These have been accompanied by a sustained campaign to bring the judiciary, governmental employees, the military and intelligence agencies, and the press into line with this new ideology and political reality.

Who forms the social base of the neo-fascist phenomenon? As a Gallup analysis and CNN exit polls have demonstrated, Trump's electoral support came mainly from the intermediate strata of the population, that is, from the lower middle class and privileged sections of the working class, primarily those with annual household incomes above the median level of around $56,000. Trump received a plurality of votes among those with incomes between $50,000 and $200,000 a year, especially in the $50,000 to $99,999 range, and among those without college degrees. Of those who reported that their financial situation was worse than four years earlier, Trump won fully 77 percent of the vote.[3] An analysis by Jonathan Rothwell and Pablo Diego-Rosell of Gallup, updated just days before the election, indicated that in contrast to standard Republican voters, much of Trump's strongest support came from relatively privileged white male workers within "skilled blue-collar industries," including "production, construction, installation, maintenance, and repair, and transportation," earning more than the median income, and over the age of forty.[4] In the so-called Rust Belt, the five states (Iowa, Michigan, Ohio, Pennsylvania, and Wisconsin) that swung the election to Trump, the Republican vote increased by over 300,000 among voters earning $50,000 or less, as compared with 2012. Meanwhile, among the same demographic, Democrats lost more than three times as many voters as the number Republicans gained.[5] None of this was enough to win Trump the national popular vote, which he lost by almost 3 million, but it gave him the edge he needed in the Electoral College.

Nationally, Trump won the white vote and the male vote by decisive margins, and gained his strongest support among rural voters. Both religious Protestants and Catholics favored the Republican presidential candidate, but his greatest support (80 percent) came from white evangelical Christians. Veterans also went disproportionately for Trump. Among those who considered immigration the nation's most pressing issue, Trump, according to CNN exit polls, received 64 percent of the vote; among those who ranked terrorism as the number-one issue, 57 percent.[6] Much of the election was dominated by both overt and indirect expressions of racism, emanating not only from the Republican nominee but also from his close associates and family (and was hardly nonexistent among the Democrats themselves). Donald Trump, Jr., in what was clearly a political ploy, repeatedly tweeted Nazi-style white supremacist slogans aimed at the far right. Trump's only slightly more veiled statements against Muslims and Mexicans, and his alliance with Breitbart, pointed in the same direction.[7]

As the Gallup report pointedly observed:

> In a study [Richard F. Hamilton, *Who Voted for Hitler*?] of perhaps the most infamous [nationalist] party, the geography of voting patterns reveals that the political supporters of Hitler's National Socialist party were disproportionately Protestants, if living in a rural area, and those in lower-middle administrative occupations and owners of small businesses, if living in an urban area. Thus, neither the rich nor poor were especially inclined to support the Nazi Party, and even among Christians, religious identity mattered greatly.[8]

The clear implication was that Trump's supporters conformed to the same general pattern. According to the Hamilton study, it is generally believed that "the lower middle class (or petty bourgeoisie) provided the decisive support for Hitler and his party."[9] Hitler also drew on a minority of the working class, disproportionately represented by more privileged blue-collar workers. But the great bulk of his support came from the lower-middle class, representing a staunchly anti-working-class, racist, and anti-establishment outlook—which nevertheless aligned itself with capital. Hitler also received backing from devout Protestants, rural voters, disabled veterans, and older voters or pensioners.[10]

The parallels with the Trump phenomenon in the United States are thus sufficiently clear. Trump's backing comes primarily neither from the working-class majority nor the capitalist class, though the latter have mostly reconciled themselves to Trumpism, given that they are its principal beneficiaries. Once in power, fascist movements have historically cleansed themselves of the more radical lower-middle-class links that helped bring them to power, and soon ally firmly with big business, a pattern already manifesting itself in the Trump administration.[11]

Yet despite these very broad similarities, key features distinguish neo-fascism in the contemporary United States from its precursors in early twentieth-century Europe. It is in many ways a unique form. There is no paramilitary violence in the streets. There are no black shirts or brown shirts, no Nazi Stormtroopers. There is, indeed, no separate fascist party.[12] Today, the world economy is dominated not by nation-based monopoly capitalism, as in classical fascism, but by a more globalized monopoly-finance capitalism.

After its defeat in the First World War, Germany in the 1930s was in the midst of the Great Depression, and about to resume its struggle for economic and imperial hegemony in Europe. In contrast, the United States today, long the world's hegemon, has been experiencing an extended period of imperial decline, coupled with economic stagnation. This represents a different trajectory. The White House's "America First" policy, unfurled in Trump's inaugural address, with its characteristically fascist "palingenetic form of ultra-nationalism" (*palingenesis* means "rebirth") is not aimed at domination of Europe and its colonies, as in Nazi Germany, but in restoring U.S. primacy over the entire world, leading to the "potentially deadliest phase of imperialism."[13]

Further distinguishing the neo-fascism of our present moment is the advent of the climate change crisis, the very reality of which the White House denies. Rather than address the problem, the new administration, backed by the fossil-capital wing of the Republican Party, has declared flatly that anthropogenic climate change does not exist. It has chosen to defy the entire world in this respect, repudiating the global scientific consensus. There are deep concerns, raised by the *Bulletin of Atomic Scientists*, which just moved its doomsday clock thirty seconds closer to midnight, that this same irrationalism may extend to nuclear weapons.[14]

But if the White House is now best described, for all of the above reasons, as neo-fascist in its leanings, this does not extend to the entire U.S. state. Congress, the courts, the civil bureaucracy, the military, the state and local governments, and what is often called, after Louis Althusser, the "ideological state apparatus"—including the media and educational institutions—would need to be brought into line before a fully neo-fascist state could operate on its own violent terms.[15] Still, there is no doubt that liberal or capitalist democracy in the United States is now endangered. At the level of the political system as a whole, we are, as political scientist Richard Falk has put it, in a "pre-fascist moment."[16] At the same time, the bases still exist within the state and civil society for organized, legal resistance.

Here it is vital to understand that fascism is not in any sense a mere political aberration or anomaly, but has historically been one of two major modes of political management adopted by ruling classes in the advanced capitalist states.[17]

Since the late nineteenth century, capitalist states, particularly those of the major imperial powers, have generally taken the form of liberal democracy—representing a kind of equilibrium between competing social sectors and tendencies, in which the capitalist class, by virtue of its control of the economy, and despite the relative autonomy accorded to the state, is able to assert its hegemony. Far from being democratic in any egalitarian sense, liberal democracy has allowed considerable room for the rise of plutocracy, that is, the rule of the rich; but it has at the same time been limited by democratic forms and rights that represent concessions to the larger population.[18] Indeed, while remaining within the boundaries of liberal democracy, the neoliberal era since the 1980s has been associated with the steepest increases in inequality in recorded history.[19]

Liberal democracy is not, however, the only viable form of rule in advanced capitalist states. In periods of systemic crisis in which property relations are threatened—such as the Great Depression of the 1930s, or the stagnation and financialization of recent decades—conditions may favor the rise of fascism. Moreover, then as now, fascism is invariably a product of the larger context of monopoly capital and imperialism, related to struggles for hegemony within the capitalist world economy. Such a crisis of world hegemony, real or perceived, fosters ultra-nationalism, racism, xenophobia, extreme protectionism, and hyper-militarism, generating repression at home and geopolitical struggle abroad. Liberal democracy, the rule of law, and the very existence of a viable political opposition may be endangered.

In such conditions, as Bertolt Brecht declared, "Contradictions are our hope!"[20] It is necessary then to ask: What are the specific contradictions of neo-fascism in the Trump era? How are they related to the larger crisis of the U.S. political economy and empire? And how do we exploit these contradictions to create a powerful, united resistance movement?

The Classical Fascist *Gleichschaltung*

"The antonym of fascism," Paul Sweezy wrote to Paul Baran in 1952, "is bourgeois democracy, not feudalism or socialism. Fascism is one of the political forms which capitalism may assume in the monopoly-imperialist phase."[21] The issue of fascism, whether in its classical or current form, thus goes beyond right-wing politics. It raises, as Baran replied to Sweezy, the much more significant question of the "jumping [off] place" that marks the qualitative break between liberal democracy and fascism (and today between neoliberalism and neo-fascism). The complete development of a fascist state, understood as a historical process, requires a seizure of the state apparatus in its totality, and therefore the elimination of any real separation of powers between the various parts, in the interest of a larger struggle for national as well as world dominance.[22] Hence, upon securing a beachhead in the government, particularly the executive, fascist interests have historically employed semi-legal means, brutality, propaganda, and intimidation as a means of integration, with big capital looking the other way or even providing direct support. In a complete fascist takeover, the already incomplete protections to individuals offered by liberal democracy are more or less eliminated, along with the forces of political opposition.

Property rights, however, are invariably protected under fascism—except for those racially, sexually, or politically targeted, whose property is often confiscated—and the interests of big capital are enhanced.[23] The political forces in power aim at what Nazi ideology called a "totalitarian state," organized around the executive, while the basic economic structure remains untouched.[24] The fascist state in its ideal conception is thus "totalitarian" in itself, reducing the political and cultural apparatus to one unitary force, but leaving the economy and the capitalist class largely free from interference, even consolidating the dominance of its monopolistic fraction.[25] The aim of the state in these circumstances is to repress and discipline the population, while protecting and promoting capitalist property relations, profits, and accumulation, and laying the basis for imperial expansion. As Mussolini declared: "The fascist regime does not intend to nationalize, or worse, bureaucratize the entire national economy, it is enough to control it and discipline it through the corporations. . . . The corporations provide the discipline and the state will only take up the sectors related to defense, the existence and security of the homeland."[26] Hitler likewise pronounced: "We stand for the maintenance of private property. . . . We shall protect free enterprise as the most expedient, or rather the sole possible economic order."[27]

Indeed, an often overlooked Nazi policy was the selling-off of state property. The concept of privatization (or re-privatization) of the economy, now a hallmark of neoliberalism, first gained currency in fascist Germany, where capitalist property relations remained sacrosanct, even as the new fascist state structure dismantled liberal-democratic institutions and instituted a war economy. At the time of Hitler's rise to power, much of the German economy was state-owned: sectors such as the steel and coal industries, shipbuilding, and banking had been largely nationalized. Under Hitler, the United Steel Trust was privatized in just a few years, and by 1937 all of the major banks were privatized. All of this increased the power and scope of capital. "The practical significance of the transference of government enterprises into private hands," Maxine Yaple Sweezy wrote in a major 1941 study of the Nazi economy, "was thus that the capitalist class continued to serve as a vessel for the accumulation of income. Profit-making and the return of property to private hands, moreover, have assisted the consolidation of Nazi Party power."[28] As Nicos Poulantzas noted in *Fascism and Dictatorship*, "Nazism maintained juridical regulation in matters of the protection of the capitalist order and private property."[29]

If privatization within industry was crucial to the rise of fascism in Germany, thereby further concentrating the economic power of the capitalist class, it was the consolidation of Nazi rule within the state itself that made the former possible, breaking the liberal-democratic order altogether. This process, known as *Gleichschaltung*—"bringing into line" or "synchronization"—defined the period of consolidation of the new political order in the years 1933–34. This meant politically integrating each of the state's separate entities, including the parliament, judiciary, civil bureaucracy, military, and the local and regional branches of government, and extending this to the major organs of the ideological state apparatus within civil society, or the educational institutions, the media, trade associations, and more.[30] This synchronization was accomplished by means of a combination of ideology, intimidation, enforced cooperation, and coercion, usually by pressuring these institutions into "cleaning their own houses." The leading Nazi jurist Carl Schmitt promoted the two principles governing *Gleichschaltung* in the German case: (1) the removal of "non-Aryans," and (2) the *Führerprinzip*—"leadership principle," placing the leader above the written laws. During this period a kind of judicial cloak legitimated the consolidation of power, to be largely dispensed with later. As Schmitt explained, the object of *Gleichschaltung* was unity and purity, achieved through the "extermination of heterogeneity."[31]

Gleichschaltung in Germany was aimed at all the separate branches of the state and the ideological state apparatus simultaneously, but underwent several stages or qualitative breaks. The Reichstag fire, set only a month after President Hindenburg's appointment of Hitler as chancellor in January 1933, prompted the issue of two executive decrees providing a legalistic justification for the violation of the constitution. These decrees were further legitimized by the Enabling Act, or "Law to Eliminate Peril to Nation and Reich," in March 1933, giving Hitler unilateral power to enact laws independent of the Reichstag. This was soon accompanied by the arrest and purging of political opponents. This period also saw the initiation of the "Law for the Restoration of the Civil Service" that allowed for the application of *Gleichschaltung* to all civil service workers. This initial stage of bringing into line ended in July 1933 with the abolition of all political parties other than the National Socialist German Workers Party.[32]

The second stage was aimed at establishing control over and integration of the military, as well as the universities, the press, and other social and cultural organizations. Not only did Hitler move to consolidate his control of the military (the *Wehrmacht*), but, in the attempt to integrate the military with the Nazi project, he declared in December 1933 that the army was "the nation's only bearer of weapons," undermining the claims of the Nazi Party's paramilitary, brown-shirt wing, the SA—*Sturmabteilung*, "Assault Division" or Stormtroopers.[33]

The "extermination of heterogeneity" within major cultural institutions is best illustrated by the absorption of the universities into Nazi doctrine. As rector of the University of Freiburg, beginning in 1933, the German philosopher Martin Heidegger was charged with the institution of *Gleichschaltung* as his main official duty. Heidegger carried out these functions to the letter, helping purge the university and denouncing colleagues. In these years, he worked closely with Carl Schmitt to promote the Nazi ideology, helping to rationalize anti-Semitism and presiding over symbolic book burnings.[34]

The third, decisive stage of *Gleichschaltung* was initiated with the bloody purge of the SA leadership from June 30 to July 2, 1934, and the subsequent establishment, particularly following Hindenburg's death that August, of Hitler as the ultimate source of law, as celebrated in Schmitt's article "The Führer Safeguards the Law." From this point on, fascist rule was consolidated in all of the main institutions of the state and the chief ideological organs of civil society.[35]

Other fascist states have followed a similar, if less totalizing, trajectory. "In the much slower process of consolidating Fascist rule in Italy," Robert O. Paxton writes in *The Anatomy of Fascism*, "only the labor unions, the political parties, and the media were fully 'brought into line.'"[36]

The Trumpist *Gleichschaltung*

Many of these developments were specific to Europe in the 1930s, and are unlikely to recur in anything resembling the same form in our day. Nevertheless, neo-fascism today also has as its aim a shift in the management of the advanced capitalist system, requiring the effective dissolution of the liberal-democratic order and its replacement by an alliance between large capital and what is now called the "alt-right," openly espousing racism, nationalism, anti-environmentalism, misogyny, homophobia, police violence, and extreme militarism.

The deeper motive of all these forms of reaction is the repression of the workforce. Behind Trump's appeals to alt-right bigotry lie the increased privatization of all state-economic functions, the reinforcement of the power of big business, and the shift to a more racially defined imperialist foreign policy. Yet to put such a neo-fascist strategy in place requires a new kind of *Gleichschaltung*, whereby various institutions—Congress, the judiciary, the civil bureaucracy, state and local governments, the military, natural security state (the "deep state"), media, and educational institutions—are all brought into line.[37]

What concrete evidence is there, then, that the Trump White House is working to implement neo-fascist forms of capitalist state management, transgressing legal norms and abrogating liberal democratic protections? Here it is useful to remind ourselves of the characteristics of fascism in general, of which U.S. neo-fascism is a specific form. As Samir Amin states in "The Return of Fascism in Contemporary Capitalism":

> The fascist choice for managing a capitalist state in crisis is always based—by definition even—on the categorical rejection of "democracy." Fascism always replaces the general principles on which the theories and practices of modern democracies are based—recognition of diversity of opinions, recourse to electoral procedures to determine a majority, guarantee of the rights of the minority, etc.—with the opposed values of submission to the requirements of collective discipline and the authority of the supreme leader and his main agents. This reversal of values is then always accompanied by a return of backward-looking ideas, which are able to provide an apparent legitimacy to the procedures of submission that are implemented. The proclamation of the supposed necessity of returning to the ("medieval") past, of submitting to the state religion or to some supposed characteristic of the "race" or the (ethnic) "nation" make up the panoply of ideological discourses deployed by the fascist powers.[38]

The ultra-nationalist and ultra-right-wing slant of the new administration is not to be doubted. In his inaugural address, written by his alt-right advisers Steve Bannon and Stephen Miller, Trump declared, in what economist Joseph Stiglitz has called "historical fascist overtones":

> From this moment on, it's going to be America First. . . . We will reinforce old alliances and form new ones—and unite the civilized world against Radical Islamic Terrorism, which we will eradicate completely from the face of the Earth. . . . We must protect our borders from the ravages of other countries making our products, stealing our companies, and destroying our jobs. . . . America will start winning again, winning like never before. . . . At the bedrock of our politics will be a total allegiance to the United States of America, and through our loyalty to our country, we will discover our loyalty to each other. When you open your heart to patriotism, there is no room for prejudice. . . . When America is united, America is totally unstoppable. There should be no fear—we are protected, and we will always be protected. We will be protected by the great men and women of our military and law enforcement and, most importantly, we are protected by God. . . . Together, We Will Make America Strong Again. We Will Make America Wealthy Again. We Will Make America Proud Again. We Will Make America Safe Again. And, Yes, Together, We Will Make America Great Again.[39]

The ideological framework and political strategy of Trumpism are chiefly the work of Bannon, formerly head of Breitbart News and now chief White House strategist, who also directed Trump's electoral campaign in its final months.[40] Bannon is flanked by two other Breitbart ideologues, Miller, a senior adviser to Trump and a protégé of Attorney General Jeff Sessions, and Sebastian Gorka, deputy assistant for national security. Another Breitbart principal,

Julia Hahn, has been appointed as a "special assistant to the president," working under Bannon as his chief assistant, and is known as "Bannon's Bannon," a polite reference to her role as an unrestrained ultra-right ideologue, hired to keep congressional Republicans in line.[41]

Bannon's neo-fascist ideology can be seen as consisting of six major components: (1) the need to overcome "the crisis of capitalism," particularly in the United States, brought on by the rise of "globalism" and "crony capitalism"; (2) the restoration of the "Judeo-Christian West" as the spiritual framework for a restored capitalism; (3) the promotion of extreme ethno-nationalism, targeting non-white immigrants; (4) an explicit identification with what he calls a "global populist movement"—that is, global neo-fascism; (5) the insistence that the United States is in a global war, a "global existential war," against "an expansionist Islam" and "an expansionist China"; and (6) the notion that the rise of the alt-right represents a quasi-mystical "great Fourth Turning" in U.S. history—after the American Revolution, the Civil War, and the Great Depression and Second World War.[42]

Bannon's ideology was most vividly on display in a 2014 talk at a Vatican conference, in which he praised the far right "populism" of France's National Front, led by Marine Le Pen, as well as Britain's UK Independence Party. He argued that "the harder-nosed the capitalism, the better." But this required a restoration of lost Judeo-Christian "spiritual and moral foundations. . . . When capitalism was . . . at its highest flower . . . almost all of those capitalists were strong believers in the Judeo-Christian West. . . . Secularism has sapped the strength of the Judeo-Christian West to defend its ideals." For Bannon, the enemy was not just liberals but the "Republican establishment" and their masters, the promoters of "crony capitalism." These were the true enemies of "middle-class people and working-class people." The racism in the movement he represented was not to be denied outright, but rather "over time it all gets kind of washed out" as people pull together in a patriotic alliance (while excluding others). All of this fits within a larger sense of a crusade: "There is a major war brewing, a war that's already global. . . . You will see we're in a war of immense proportions."[43]

Most remarkable was the sympathetic way that Bannon, fielding questions after his talk, called upon the ideas of the Italian fascist Julius Evola, a source of inspiration to and supporter of Mussolini, and later of Hitler, who emerged after the Second World War as a leading figure in the Traditionalist movement of European neo-fascism, making him a hero of the alt-right white supremacist leader Richard Spencer in the United States.[44] In the 1930s, Evola declared, "*Fascism is too little.* We would have wanted a fascism which is more radical, more intrepid, a fascism that is truly absolute, made of pure force, unavailable for any compromise. . . . We would never be considered anti-fascist, except to the extent that super-fascism would be equivalent to anti-fascism." In his postwar writings, he argued that Traditionalists "should not accept the adjective 'fascist' or 'neo-fascist' *tout court*," but rather they should emphasize only their "positive" characteristics, allying themselves with the "aristocratic" values of the European tradition. The goal was the creation of a new, spiritual "European *Imperium* . . . We must create a unity of fighters." The ultimate intent was the resurrection of traditional sovereignty understood as the spiritual power of a nation, or *patria* (fatherland).[45]

Bannon, himself a strong promoter of "palingenetic ultra-nationalism," in tune with Evola, argued that those in the Judeo-Christian West needed to resurrect "traditionalism . . . particularly the sense of where it supports the underpinnings of nationalism." Most important, he told his audience at the Vatican, was the restoration of the "long history of the Judeo-Christian West's struggle against Islam." Speaking of sovereignty in Evola's sense, Bannon stated: "I think that people, particularly in certain countries, want to see sovereignty for their country, they want to see nationalism for their country." But as he made clear, this first required the deconstruction of the political "governing class" and of the state in its current form.[46]

Insofar as the Trump White House sees itself as empowered to unleash a neo-fascist strategy of *Gleichschaltung*, along the general lines suggested above, one would expect to see an assault on the major branches of the state and the ideological state apparatus, transgressing legal and political norms and seeking to vastly increase the power of the presidency. Indeed, much early evidence suggests that the political culture has changed in this respect in the brief period that the administration has been in power. All the major sectors of the state have come under attack. The most extreme action was Trump's January 27 executive order immediately banning immigrants from seven predominantly Muslim countries in the Middle East, which, in the face of national protests, was quickly overturned by the federal courts. This led Trump to issue personal attacks on individual judges, in an effort to delegitimize them in the eyes of his supporters, a move that could be seen as a preliminary attempt to bring the judiciary into line.[47]

These events were followed in February by Trump's executive order establishing a quasi-legal basis for the mass deportation of an estimated eleven million undocumented individuals in the United States—even long-term residents and those never convicted of any crime, and without reference to age. This was to be complemented by the administration's long-promised construction of what the president called, in his February 28 address to Congress, "a great, great wall along our southern border." In this legal and political morass,

Trump is inheriting 103 judicial vacancies, nearly twice the number inherited by Obama, giving the new administration the ability to restructure the judiciary in ways likely to remove constitutional rights and reinforce repression.[48]

Trump's conflict with the national security state or "intelligence community," consisting of hundreds of thousands of employees across seventeen agencies, began almost immediately, and was prefaced by his repeated attacks on the intelligence agencies while running for office. In late January, he issued a directive—later reversed—reorganizing the National Security Council (NSC) and the Homeland Security Council (HSC), in which the CIA director, the director of national intelligence, and the chairman of the Joint Chiefs of Staff were removed from the regular members of the NSC and HSC Principals Committee; and, in another break with precedent, Bannon, the White House chief strategist, was added to the Principals Committee. A popular backlash prompted the administration partially to backtrack, restoring the CIA director as a member of the Principals Committee and eventually removing Bannon from that role, but the intention of undermining the existing structure of authority within the national security state was clear.[49]

The Trump administration's attempts to destabilize and bring into line the national security state provoked a countervailing response in the form of a proliferation of leaks within the "deep state" that within a few weeks brought down Michael Flynn, Trump's initial pick as National Security Adviser—partly due to conflict with Vice President Pence and more traditional Republicans. Tensions were further inflamed by Trump and Bannon's sudden move to shift the United States' geopolitical posture away from the New Cold War with Russia and toward a global battle against "radical Islam" and China. Although he has peppered his administration with generals in order to integrate with the military,

Trump remains locked in conflict with much of the national security state.

Nor is the rest of the state free from such efforts to bring it into line. There are more than 2.7 million civilian employees in the federal government. Trump supporter Newt Gingrich stated that "ninety-five percent of the bureaucrats are against him." Longtime Republican operative and Trump strategist Roger Stone has said that "there aren't that many Trump loyalists in the White House," necessitating a rapid change in personnel. Press leaks from within the state convinced Trump supporters that the most pressing task was to accelerate the removal of civilian employees not in line with the new administration. According to Newsmax CEO Chris Ruddy, Trump's close friend and adviser, "The federal bureaucracy itself is a powerful machine, and they tend to have very establishment ideas"—meaning opposed to the new alt-right agenda.[50]

This is part of a more general attack on the civil bureaucracy. Bannon has declared that a "new political order" is imminent, promoting "economic nationalism" and entailing the "deconstruction of the administrative state." The administration, he says, will be in a constant battle for "deconstruction."[51] The undermining of the civilian bureaucracy has been most pronounced in the environmental agencies, mostly because there whole departments can be brought under the ax. In a meeting with business leaders shortly after his inauguration, Trump indicated that his administration planned to cut governmental regulations on business by "75 percent," and "maybe more."[52] Beyond financial deregulation, the plan is to go after environmental regulations in particular, along with environmentalists within the federal bureaucracy.

Myron Ebell, head of the Competitive Enterprise Institute, a major organ for climate denial, and a key Trump adviser on the environment, has declared the environmental movement "the greatest threat to freedom and prosperity in the modern world" and has attacked climate scientists and other members of what he calls the "expertariat," with the aim of removing them from government.[53] Ebell has gone so far as to characterize the Pope's encyclical on climate change as "leftist drivel."[54] This anti-establishment rhetoric, so integral to the success of Trump's campaign, is now being used to legitimize cuts of 20–25 percent in the Environmental Protection Agency (EPA) budget and 17 percent in the National Oceanic and Atmospheric Administration.

A sweeping purge in areas of the federal government related to environmental protection is expected, with whole agencies directed at issues like climate change eliminated and employees bullied into compliancy. The recent Republican congressional revival of a defunct 1876 law that would allow the salaries of federal employees to be reduced to $1 a year is being wielded as a weapon to threaten governmental employees.[55]

Cornel West has spoken of the "repressive apparatus" that defines the Trump administration. "That's the neo-fascist dimension of it. It's not just the attack on the press," West told his audience at Harvard's W. E. B. DuBois Institute. "He will be coming for some of us. We have to say, like DuBois, like Frederick Douglass, and like the nameless and anonymous freedom fighters of all colors, we can stand [up].... I refuse to normalize Donald Trump and his neo-fascist project."[56] How and at what speed the new administration will unleash this repression is still unclear, though the massive scale of the deportations of undocumented immigrants—projected to be far greater than those under Obama—and the scarcely veiled racism that animates them, is already evident. There is little doubt that the Trump administration will reinforce the "new Jim Crow" system of racialized mass incarceration. He has insisted on the need for further privatization of federal prisons, something already being introduced into policy by Sessions. Before Trump's election, as many as 141,000 people signed a petition sent to the Obama White House—heavily promoted by Breitbart—requesting that Black Lives Matter be listed as a terrorist organization. Trump, himself, insisted, prior to the election, that Black Lives Matter was a "threat" and that the U.S. attorney general should be asked to do something about it, starting with "watching, because that's really bad stuff," which suggested the need for massive surveillance. He has also come out for expanded racial profiling by police across the country.[57]

At the same time, an assault is being prepared on labor unions, in particular public-sector unions. The Republican Congress, bolstered by Trump, is proposing a national "right-to-work" law aimed at stripping unions of their funding by making it possible for workers to be free riders, receiving the benefits of union bargaining without having to pay the "agency fees" to support it, with the result that the unions are to be driven into a financial crisis. Right-to-work laws already exist in twenty-seven states. The U.S. Supreme Court, with a restored conservative majority, may achieve much the same result even more quickly in upcoming court decisions, stripping public-sector unions of their ability to deduct agency fees from the paychecks of workers covered by the union agreement. School privatization is likewise aimed directly at breaking teachers' unions. The overall goal is to end *de facto*, if not *de jure*, workers' rights to organize in the United States.[58] Though Trump's first choice for labor secretary, fast-food mogul Andrew Puzder, was forced to withdraw amid popular protest and Republican discomfort, his nomination was fully in line with this labor-crushing campaign. Puzder was found to have consistently ignored and violated wage, safety, and overtime laws in his fast-food conglomerate, CKE Restaurants. In Puzder's place, Trump chose the current secretary of labor, R. Alexander Acosta, a former member of George W. Bush's National Labor Relations Board who went on to become assistant attorney general in the Justice Department's Civil Rights division in the Bush administration. Acosta's singular response to all tough questions in his confirmation hearings was that he would simply follow the orders of Trump, whom he regarded as his boss.[59]

Trump's education secretary, billionaire Betsy DeVos, who has long been dedicated to the privatization of public education, represents an assault on a bedrock of democracy in the United States. DeVos is a strong supporter of charter schools and school vouchers aimed at the demolition of the entire public education system in the United States, which she has dismissed as a "dead end." The federal government provides relatively little money to public K-12 education, which is mostly funded by state and local governments. Most federal money is devoted to helping students with disabilities and those from low-income communities. Trump, however, has vowed to fund vouchers massively nationwide in a proposal that assumes that states will kick in more than $100 billion for vouchers, taking that directly from public education. Trump's choice of DeVos indicates that the emphasis in the new administration will be on promoting maximum privatization of U.S. public education, which would lead to vastly increased disparities in access to education and destroy teachers' unions and teacher professionalism. But DeVos has objectives beyond that. She has stated that in privatizing the schools "our desire is to confront the culture in ways that will continue to advance God's kingdom."[60]

The Trump administration's effort to bring universities into line was evident in the new president's response to a riot that occurred on the UC-Berkeley campus in early February, when protestors clashed with police, prompting the cancellation of a speech by Milo Yiannopoulos, then a Breitbart senior editor (and close Bannon associate) known for his white supremacist, misogynist hate speech. After Yiannopoulos's talk was canceled, Trump tweeted that Berkeley should be denied federal funds.[61] Trump's election has fueled right-wing attacks on universities. Days after his election, the right-wing nonprofit Turning Point USA announced the creation of a "Professor Watchlist" targeting more than two hundred professors in the United States (including me) as dangerous progressives to be "watched"—a move designed to intimidate the universities.

The new administration is marked by an extraordinary attempt to bring the mainstream media in line with its neo-fascist objectives. Trump has declared that he is in a "running war" with the media and that journalists are "among the most dishonest people on earth." Barely a month into his presidency, Trump tweeted that the mainstream media "is the enemy of the American people" and that the *New York Times*, NBC News, ABC, CBS, and CNN were all "FAKE NEWS."[62] These were not of course rational attacks on the mainstream capitalist media for what Edward Herman and Noam Chomsky called its "propaganda model"—or the systematic day-to-day filtering of news in order to promote capitalism and its power elite, while at the same time excluding or marginalizing all left criticisms. Rather, Trump was disparaging the non-Murdoch mainstream media for its general defense of separation of powers and civil liberties.[63] This included the media's questioning of Trump's claim that he only lost the popular vote in the election due to voter fraud, its coverage of his ban on immigration from seven predominantly Muslim countries, and its treatment of the new administration's contacts with Russia.

In an alarming display of Goebbels-like tactics, Bannon told the press to "shut up" in a press conference in January, and declared, "The media here is the opposition party. . . .

The media has zero integrity, zero intelligence, and no hard work." He further ranted, "You're the opposition party. Not the Democratic Party. You're the opposition party. The media's the opposition party." For Bannon, this "opposition party" has to be completely brought into line. The object, as noted by the *New York Times*, is to so manipulate and intimidate the media that it will "muzzle itself."[64]

In an extraordinary instance of *Gleichschaltung*, the Trump-dominated Republican Party issued a "Mainstream Media Accountability Survey," rife with leading questions, misleading "facts," and ideological posturing, which the usually staid National Public Radio called "phenomenally biased."[65] This was soon followed by the exclusion of the *New York Times*, CNN, Politico, BuzzFeed, and other media from a White House press briefing, due to their unfavorable stories on the Trump administration (the Associated Press and *Time* refused to attend in protest).[66] Bannon's *Gleichschaltung* strategy is also aimed at the traditional right itself. Thus, in December 2016 he declared, "*National Review* and *The Weekly Standard* are both left-wing magazines, and I want to destroy them also."[67]

As part of a general ideological campaign, Bannon's attacks on the media, in what is a long-standing technique of fascist and neo-fascist "radicals," borrows from the language of the left, referring to "the corporatist, globalist media" as the enemy. Yet the real ideological driving force of neo-fascism is the ultra-nationalist one of the resurrection of a national-racial culture. Thus Bannon has spoken in Evola-like terms of the United States as "a nation with a culture and a reason for being," creating a distinct principle of "sovereignty."[68] The concept of the restoration of national "sovereignty" has become a key organizing principle of the alt-right ideology promoted by Breitbart and has been employed to justify the anti-immigrant stance of the Trump White House.[69]

Part of the power of the Trump administration lies in a largely compliant and ideologically right-wing Republican-dominated Congress. But the *Gleichschaltung* extends to the Republican Party leadership too, the chief figures of which are being bullied into line. An indication of this is Bannon's hiring of Breitbart's Julia Hahn, known for her unrestrained attacks on Paul Ryan and other leading Republicans, as his assistant—thereby warning the Republican leadership of what could await them if they were to refuse to play ball. Hahn made her reputation by accusing Ryan of fleeing "grieving moms trying to show him photos of their children killed by his open borders agenda." She charged Ryan of being a "globalist" linked to crony capitalism, and as the mastermind of a "months-long campaign to elect Hillary Clinton." Here the *Gleichschaltung* strategy aimed at the Republican Party itself is quite clear: "A number of House Republicans told the *Washington Post* that Hahn's involvement signaled Bannon's plans to possibly put her to use against them, writing searing commentaries about elected Republican leaders to ram through Trump's legislative priorities and agitate the party's base if necessary."[70]

What makes the rise of a neo-fascist White House of such great concern is the enormous weight of the U.S. presidency, and the long-term breakdown in the separation of powers in the U.S. Constitution. The undermining of the congressional power to declare war, established in the Constitution, is well known. Moreover, with the Patriot Act and other measures, the power of the executive branch has been greatly expanded so far this century. In his statement in signing the National Defense Authorization Act for 2011, Obama affirmed that the executive branch now has the power of "indefinite military detention without trial of American citizens," removing thereby the protections of the courts and individual rights established in the Constitution. This means an enormous extension of the power of the presidency against that of the judiciary, continuing a process of the abrogation of judicial review in expanding areas of "national security," which has seriously undermined the separation of powers in the U.S. Constitution. Such power conferred on the presidency makes conceivable an abrupt shift of the state in a dictatorial direction, ostensibly under the rule of law. Although Obama in 2011 indicated that he would not authorize military detention without trial of U.S. citizens, which he said "would break with our most important traditions and values as a nation," he did not question the legal right of a future president to do so, or fight against this provision within the law, which abrogated the constitutional protections of citizens. With the advent of what Bill Moyers and Michael Winship have called a virtual "coup" in the executive branch of government, there is much less assurance that the White House will exercise restraint in this area.[71]

Trump and the Decline of U.S. Hegemony

Trump was elected to the presidency on a pledge to "Make America Great Again." Following the ideological template offered by Bannon and Breitbart, he pointed to the reality of continuing economic crisis or slow growth, high unemployment, the deteriorating economic conditions of the working class, and the weakening of the United States in the world as a whole. His answer was economic and military nationalism, "draining the swamp" (the end of crony capitalism in Washington), and attacks on big government. All of this was laced with misogyny, racism, and xenophobia. Among Trump's pledges was an end to economic stagnation, with the newly elected president promising an annual growth rate of 4 percent, compared to just 1.6 percent in 2016.[72] He declared he would create jobs through massive infrastructure spending, elimination of trade agreements unfavorable to the United States, spurring investment by cutting taxes and regulations, and colossal increases in military spending—at the same time protecting entitlements such as Social Security and Medicare.

After years of feeling ignored by the dominant neoliberal ideology, large numbers of those in the white, and particularly male, population who saw themselves as lower-middle class or relatively better-off working class rallied to Trump's economic nationalist, overtly racist cause—though of course few had any real notion of what this would fully entail.[73] The fact that the Democratic Party nominated Hillary Clinton, the very image of neoliberalism, over Bernie Sanders, with his grassroots social-democratic candidacy, played into the Trump-Breitbart strategy.

Trump also drew considerable support in the election from the "billionaire class," particularly within the FIRE (finance, insurance, and real estate) and energy sectors, which saw his promises on cutting corporate taxes, increasing federal financing of private firms in infrastructure developments, and promoting economic nationalism, as ways of leveraging their own positions. After the election Wall Street's support turned to elation with stocks rising rapidly. Between Trump's win and February 24, the Dow and Nasdaq both rose by 13 percent, Standard and Poor's by 10 percent. Most of the enthusiasm was for expected tax cuts and massive deregulation.[74] According to the London-based *Financial Times*, "Donald Trump is creating a field day for the one percent." Meanwhile, his repeated promises of infrastructure investment to create jobs for the working population were being revealed as largely fraudulent, a case of "bait and switch."[75]

Although it is true that Trump still promises a $1 trillion investment in the nation's physical infrastructure, this was never meant to take the form of direct federal spending. Rather, Trump's commerce secretary, Wilbur Ross Jr., is the author of a highly questionable report claiming that tax credits to corporations on the order of $137 billion would provide the financing for private companies to leverage $1 trillion in infrastructure spending over ten years. The entire plan, as concocted by Ross, rests not on governmental spending on infrastructure, but rather on giving capital back to capital: a huge windfall to private contractors, much of it subsidizing projects that would have occurred anyway.[76]

Trump promised to fight crony capitalism and to "drain the swamp," but has filled his cabinet with billionaires and Wall Street insiders, making it clear that the state would do the bidding of monopoly-finance capital. Ross has assets valued at $2.9 billion, and was designated by *Forbes* as a "vulture" and a "king of bankruptcy." DeVos, secretary of education, is worth $5.1 billion, while her brother, Erik Prince, called by Intercept "America's most notorious mercenary" and a Trump adviser, was the founder of the universally hated Blackwater security firm. Steven Mnuchin, Trump's treasury secretary, is a cento-millionaire hedge fund investor. Rex Tillerson, the new secretary of state, is the former CEO of ExxonMobil. Trump's initial seventeen cabinet picks (a number of whom were forced to drop out from consideration) had a combined wealth that exceeded that of a third of the population of the country. This does not include Trump's own wealth, currently in the billions. Never before has there been so pure a plutocracy, so extreme an example of crony capitalism, in any U.S. administration.[77]

What paved the way for Trump's neo-fascist strategy and gave it coherence was the deepening long-term crisis of U.S. political economy and empire, and of the entire world capitalist economy, after the financial crisis of 2007–2009. This left the system in a state of economic stagnation, with no visible way out. The financialization process, characterized by expanding debt leverage and market bubbles, which in the 1980s and '90s had helped lift the economy out of a malaise resulting from the overaccumulation of capital, was no longer viable on the scale needed.

In 2012, I published *The Endless Crisis* with Robert W. McChesney, based on articles that appeared in *Monthly Review* between 2009 and 2012. In the opening paragraph, we observed:

> The Great Financial Crisis and the Great Recession arose in the United States in 2007 and quickly spread around the globe, marking what appears to be a turning point in world history. Although this was followed within two years by a recovery phase, the world economy five years after the onset of the crisis is still in the doldrums. The United States, Europe, and Japan remain caught in a condition of slow growth, high unemployment, and financial instability, with new economic tremors appearing all the time and the effects spreading globally. The one bright spot in the world economy, from a global standpoint, has been the seemingly unstoppable expansion of a handful of emerging economies, particularly China. Yet the continuing stability of China is now also in question. Hence, the general consensus among informed economic observers is that the world capitalist economy is facing the threat of long-term economic stagnation (complicated by the prospect of further financial deleveraging), sometimes referred to as the problem of "lost decades." It is this issue, of the stagnation of the capitalist economy, even more than that of financial crisis or recession, that has now emerged as the big question worldwide.[78]

Five years later, this "big question" has in no sense gone away.

Economic stagnation is endemic. As the *Financial Times* acknowledged in February 2017 in an article questioning the stagnation thesis, "the secular speed limit on growth in the advanced economies is still much lower than it was in earlier decades."[79] The U.S. economy has had only a meager 2.1 percent average annual growth rate since the end of the Great Recession in 2010. The country has now experienced more than a decade of less than 3 percent growth, for the first time since growth rates began to be recorded in the early 1930s—a period that includes the Great Depression.[80] The labor share of income of all but the top 1 percent has been declining dramatically.[81] Net investment, which normally drives the economy, is stagnant and in long-term decline.[82] Unemployment rates, while seemingly low at the beginning of 2017 are, as the economy approaches the peak of the business cycle, being kept down largely as a result of millions of people leaving the workforce, together with an enormous increase in part-time work and precarious jobs.[83] Income and wealth inequality in the society meanwhile have been soaring. U.S. household debt, now at $12.6 trillion, is the highest in a decade. Despite an aging population, homeownership in the United States is at its lowest level since 1965.[84]

Nor are these conditions confined to the United States. The G7 richest countries of Canada, France, Germany, Italy, Japan, United Kingdom, and United States, taken together, saw an average rate of growth in 2016 of 1.3 percent, capping a long period of slow growth. The European Union had a growth rate of only 1.7 percent over the last decade, 1.8 percent in the last year. (To put these figures in perspective, the average annual growth rate of the U.S. economy in the depression decade from 1929 to 1939 was 1.3 percent.)[85]

These economic conditions are accompanied by the shift of production from the Global North to the Global South, where about 70 percent of industrial production now takes place as opposed to around 50 percent in 1980.[86] Although today's monopoly-finance capital in the North continues to siphon vast economic surpluses from the South via multinational corporations, including financial institutions, these surpluses for the most part no longer feed production in the North but simply add to the gross profit margins of companies, stimulating financial-asset accumulation. Hence there is a growing disconnection between record wealth concentration at the top of the society and income generation within the overall economy.[87] All of the major economies of the triad of the United States and Canada, Europe, and Japan have seen the share of income going to the top 1 percent skyrocket since 1980—rising by more than 120 percent in the United States between 1980 and 2015, even as the economy increasingly fell prey to stagnation. The top decile of wealth holders in the United States now holds more than 70 percent of the wealth of the country, while the bottom half's share is virtually nil. The six wealthiest billionaires in the world, four of whom are Americans, now own more wealth than the bottom half of the world's population.[88]

In the United States, these global shifts are further complicated by the slow decline of U.S. hegemony, which is now reaching a critical stage. With the U.S. economy currently growing at a 1.6 percent rate and the Chinese economy growing, despite its slowdown, by around 7 percent, the writing is on the wall for U.S. hegemony in the world economy. The U.S. share in the global economy has fallen steadily since 2000. In 2016 *Forbes* announced that the Chinese economy will likely overtake the U.S. economy in overall size by 2018.[89] Although the United States is a far richer country, with a much higher per capita income, the significance of this shift, and of the more general erosion of U.S. hegemony according to a wide array of indicators, is now the main global concern of the U.S. power structure. The United States retains financial hegemony, including the dominance of the dollar as the world's leading currency, and is still by far the world's leading military power. But history suggests that neither of these can be maintained in coming decades without hegemony in global production. The Obama-era strategy of trying to maintain economic hegemony not simply through U.S. power alone, but also through the power of the triad, is failing, due to economic stagnation throughout the advanced capitalist economies in the United States and Canada, Europe and Japan. This has fed a more economic-nationalist outlook in both the United States and United Kingdom.

Meanwhile, the restructuring of the U.S. economy in the context of its declining global hegemony has contributed to the widespread impression that its diminishing global power—dramatized by its endless and seemingly futile wars in the Middle East, which produce few victories—is the source of all the pain and hardship endured by the lower-middle and working classes.[90] Foreigners "taking U.S. jobs" and immigrants working for low wages have thus become easy targets, feeding an ultra-right nationalism that is useful to those in power, and that merges with the concerns of part of the ruling class.[91] The result is not only the growth of Trumpism in the United States, but Brexit in Britain, and far-right movements throughout the European core. As Amin has written:

> The following phenomena are inextricably linked to one another: the capitalism of oligopolies; the political power of oligarchies; barbarous globalization; financialization; U.S. hegemony [now declining and therefore even more dangerous]; the militarization of the way globalization operates in the service of the oligopolies; the decline of democracy; the plundering of the planet's resources; and the abandoning of development for the South.[92]

More recently, Amin has called this the problem of "generalized monopoly capitalism."[93]

All fascist or neo-fascist movements emphasize extreme nationalism, xenophobia, and racism, and are concerned with defending borders and expanding power by military means. What is known as geopolitics, or the attempt to leverage imperial power in the world through control of wider portions of the globe and their strategic resources, arose in the imperialist struggles at the beginning of the twentieth century, as articulated in the work of its classic theorists, Halford Mackinder in Britain, Karl Haushofer in Germany, and Nicholas John Spykman in the United States, and can be regarded as inherent to monopoly capitalism in all of its phases.[94] Beginning with the 1990–91 Gulf War and its immediate aftermath, U.S. geopolitics has been aimed at restoring and entrenching U.S. hegemony in the wake of the disappearance of the Soviet Union from the world stage—making the United States the sole superpower. As articulated by U.S. strategists in the early 1990s, such as Paul Wolfowitz, the goal was to take advantage of the limited amount of time—Wolfowitz saw it as a decade or at most two—before a new, rival superpower could be expected to arise, during which the United States could freely carry out regime change in the Middle East and North Africa, and along the periphery of the former Soviet Union.[95]

This approach led to a series of U.S.-led wars and regime change in the Middle East, Eastern Europe, and North Africa. The Persian Gulf in particular was a priority, of vital strategic value not only geographically but because of its immense oil resources. But gaining control of all of Eastern Europe and weakening Russia was also crucial.

The push of NATO into Ukraine, supporting a right-wing coup in the attempt to check Russia as a reemerging superpower, led to a Russian pushback under Vladimir Putin, with the annexation of the Crimea and intervention in Ukraine along its borders. Russia further responded by aggressively intervening in Syria, undermining the attempt by the United States, NATO, and Saudi Arabia to bring down the Assad regime through their support of surrogate pro-Salafist forces (committed to the creation of a fundamentalist Sunni state). Meanwhile, the destruction of Iraq in U.S.-led wars, and the Western and Gulf-state promotion of pro-Salafist armies in the context of the surrogate war in Syria, combined to bring about the rise of the Islamic State.[96]

These grim facts, representing what Richard Haass, head of the Council of Foreign Relations, has called "a world in disarray," have opened a rift within the ruling class over U.S. geopolitical strategy.[97] The main part of the ruling class and the national security state was strongly committed to a New Cold War with Russia. In accord with this, Hillary Clinton vowed, if elected president, to introduce no-fly zones in Syria, which would have meant shooting down Russian as well as Syrian planes, bringing the world to the brink of global thermonuclear war. In contrast, Trump initially put his emphasis on a détente with Russia so that the United States could concentrate on a global war against "radical Islamic terrorism" and a cold-hot war against China, in line with Bannon's Judeo-Christian war—resembling Samuel Huntington's notion of the "clash of civilizations."[98] Here Islamophobia merges with China-phobia—and with Latino-phobia, as represented by the so-called defense of the U.S. southern border.

In the Trump vision of the restoration of U.S. geopolitical and economic power, enemies are primarily designated in racial and religious terms. A renewed emphasis is put on placing U.S. boots on the ground in the Middle East and on a naval confrontation with China in the South China Sea, where much of the world's new oil reserves are to be found, and which is China's main future surety of access to oil in the case of world conflict. However, the result of this attempt to institute a sudden shift in the geopolitical strategy of the United States has been not only a falling-out in the U.S. ruling class between neoliberals (and neoconservatives) and Trump-style neo-fascists, but also a struggle within the deep state, resulting in the leaks that brought down Flynn.[99]

Trump's geopolitical strategy ultimately looks east toward China, taking the form of threatened protectionism combined with military posturing. The new administration immediately moved to set aside the Trans-Pacific Partnership, which appeared to be failing as an instrument for controlling China—preferring instead blunter methods, including a possible confrontation with China over the South China Sea.

Overlaying all of this is Trump's declaration that the United States is about to enter one of the "greatest military buildups in American history." In his budget he has indicated he intends to increase military spending by $54 billion or by around 10 percent of the Pentagon's current base budget.[100] This is likely to be seen also as a means of absorbing economic surplus, since the vast infrastructure spending promised in the presidential election is unlikely to materialize given traditional Republican party resistance. (As indicated above, the Trump plan to provide tax credits to industry for infrastructure spending will do little directly to stimulate the economy.)

Can Trump succeed economically? An analysis in the *Financial Times* at the end of February suggests that "the effect of Mr. Trump's economic agenda will be to deepen the conditions that gave rise to his candidacy."[101] Given the secular stagnation in the economy, and the structural basis of this in the overaccumulation of capital, any attempt to put the U.S. economy on another trajectory is fraught with difficulties.

Former Treasury Secretary Larry Summers writes: "I would put the odds of a U.S. recession at about 1/3 over the next year and at over 1/2 over the next 2 years."[102] Coming along after a lost decade of deep economic stagnation, including an extremely slow economic recovery, this would likely be experienced as calamitous throughout the society.

Against this one has to recall that it was Hitler who first introduced Keynesian economic stimulus through military spending, privatization, and breaking unions, instituting deep cuts in workers' wages.[103] A neo-fascist economic strategy would be a more extreme version of neoliberal austerity, backed by racism and war preparation. It would be aimed at liberating capital from regulation—giving free rein to monopoly-finance capital. This would be accompanied by more aggressive attempts to wield U.S. power directly, on a more protectionist basis. In the longer run the economic contradictions of the system would remain, but the new economic nationalism would be aimed at making sure that in the context of global economic stagnation the United States would seize a greater share of the global pie. Nevertheless, an expansion of the war economy is fraught with dangers, and its stimulus effects on production are less potent than in the past.[104] There is no surety that the United States would win a trade and currency war or a global arms race, and such developments could presage the kind of rising conflict that historically has led to world war.

The Resistible Rise of Donald Trump

Brecht's 1941 satirical play *The Resistible Rise of Arturo Ui* was an allegorical attempt to place Hitler's rise in Germany in the more familiar context—at least to American audiences—of Chicago gangsterism (in this case, a mob-controlled cauliflower monopoly), so as to suggest how fascism might be prevented in the future. Brecht's main point, apart from stripping the Nazi protagonists of any traces of greatness, was that the fascistization of society was a process, and that if the nature of the fascist techniques of gaining power, by means of propaganda, violence, threats, intimidation, and betrayal, were better understood at an early stage and by the population in general, they could be countered through a conscious movement from below. Fascism, Brecht believed, was bound to be defeated, but the continuation of capitalism ensured its reemergence: "The womb he [Ui, or Hitler] crawled from is still growing strong."[105]

Given the reality of the penetration of neo-fascism into the White House, knowledge of the process of "bringing into line" that is now being attempted by the executive branch, is essential in organizing a systematic defense of the separation of powers and constitutional freedoms. But in resisting the U.S. alt-right, the old Popular Front strategy of the left uniting with establishment liberalism is only practical to a limited extent in certain areas, such as combating climate change, which threatens all of humanity, or in efforts to protect basic political rights. This is because, short of real structural change, any initial gains achieved through such an alliance are likely soon to be abrogated once the immediate crisis is over, causing the old contradictions to reappear. An effective resistance movement against the right thus requires the construction of a powerful anti-capitalist movement from below, representing an altogether different solution, aimed at epoch-making structural change. Here the object is overturning the logic of capital, and promoting substantive equality and sustainable human development.[106] Such a revolt must be directed not just against neo-fascism, but against neoliberalism—that is, monopoly-finance capital—as well. It must be as concerned with the struggles against racism, misogyny, xenophobia, oppression of LGBTQ people, imperialism, war, and ecological degradation, as much as it is with class exploitation, necessitating the building of a broad unified movement for structural change, or a new *movement toward socialism*.

The worse thing in present circumstances would be if we were to trivialize or downplay the entry of neo-fascism into the White House or the relation of this to capitalism, imperial expansion, and global exterminism (climate change and the growing dangers of thermonuclear war). In his statement for International Holocaust Remembrance Day, Trump, while pointedly failing to mention the killing of six million Jews, declared, in Manichean terms: "It is impossible to fathom the depravity and horror inflicted on innocent people by Nazi terror.… As we remember those who died, we are deeply grateful to those who risked their lives to save the innocent. . . . I pledge to do everything in my power throughout my Presidency, and my life, to ensure that the forces of evil never again defeat the powers of good."[107]

More than three decades ago, left historian Basil Davidson concluded his *Scenes from the Anti-Nazi War* with these words:

> Now, in our own time, the old contest [fascism versus the democratic resistance] is there again. Self-appointed super-patriots of the far right . . . croak their froglike voices to the tunes of a victory which, they would have us believe, was theirs: whereas, in fact, the truth was precisely the reverse. New "national fronts" clamber on the scene, no smaller or more stupid than the Nazis were when they began. Old equivocations are replaced by new equivocations, just as apparently "respectable and proper" as the old ones were.
>
> They are all things to resist. Now as then: but sooner this time. A lot sooner.[108]

This Is Not Populism

> I am concerned with power politics—that is to say, I make use of all means that seem to me to be of service, without the slightest concern for the proprieties or for codes of honor.
>
> —Adolf Hitler[1]

The rise of Donald Trump to president of the United States is commonly thought to represent the triumph of "right-wing populism," or simply "populism." The term populism is notoriously difficult to define, since lacking any definite substantive content.[2] It is used in the dominant discourse to refer to any movement that appeals to "the people," while attacking "the elites."[3] In the United States, populism has a much older history associated with the great agrarian revolt of the late nineteenth century.[4] But today the concept primarily has to do with the growth in Europe, and more recently in the United States, of so-called right-wing populism—and only secondarily with what are labeled left-wing populist movements, such as Syriza in Greece, Podemos in Spain, or Occupy in the United States.

Right-wing populism is a euphemism introduced into the European discussion in the last few decades to refer to movements in the "fascist genus" (fascism/neo-fascism/post-fascism), characterized by virulently xenophobic, ultra-nationalist tendencies, rooted primarily in the lower-middle class and relatively privileged sections of the working class, in alliance with monopolistic capital.[5] This can be seen in the National Front in France, the Northern League in Italy, the Party for Freedom in the Netherlands, the UK Independence Party, the Sweden Democrats, and similar parties and movements in other advanced capitalist countries.[6]

The same basic phenomenon has now triumphed in the United States, in the form of Trump's rise to chief executive. Yet mainstream commentary has generally avoided the question of fascism or neo-fascism in this context, preferring instead to apply the vaguer, safer notion of populism. This is not just because of the horrific images of Nazi Germany and the Holocaust that the term fascist evokes, or because it has been increasingly used as an all-purpose term of political abuse. Rather, the liberal mainstream's aversion to the neo-fascist designation arises principally from the critique of capitalism that any serious engagement with this political phenomenon would entail. As Bertolt Brecht asked in 1935: "How can anyone tell the truth about Fascism, unless he is willing to speak out against capitalism, which brings it forth?"[7]

In today's political context, it is crucial to understand not only how the failures of neoliberalism give rise to neo-fascism, but also to connect these developments to the structural crisis of monopoly-finance capital—that is, to the regime of concentrated, financialized, and globalized capitalism. Only based on such a thoroughgoing historical critique is it possible to conceive the necessary forms of resistance.

The Cloak of Populism

The notion of right-wing populism is employed in liberal discourse as a mildly negative epithet; one that both decries this tendency, and at the same time offers it a cloak—by setting aside the whole question of fascism/neo-fascism. This reflects the ruling class's ambiguous relation to the "radical right," which, for all its supposed "radicalism," is recognized as fully compatible with capitalism. Indeed, the forces of the neo-fascist right, though still regarded warily by global elites, have been systematically "de-demonized" in much of Europe, and are often seen as acceptable partners in a center-right (or right-center) government.[8]

The Trump phenomenon is now undergoing a comparable assimilation. Historians Federico Finchelstein and Pablo Piccato wrote in a recent *Washington Post* op-ed that "racism and charismatic leadership bring Trump close to the fascist equation but he might be better described as post-fascist, which is to say populist. . . . Modern populism arose from the defeat of fascism, [and] as a novel post-fascist attempt to bring back the fascist experience to the democratic path, creating in turn an authoritarian form of democracy." Other mainstream commentators are even more allergic to any association of the Trump phenomenon with fascism. Thus Vox writer Dylan Matthews insists, "Trump is not a fascist. . . . He's a right-wing populist." Most pundits deftly avoid the question altogether. For *New York Times* columnist Thomas Edsall, Trump represents "the ascendance of right-wing populism in America," plain and simple.[9]

The hegemonic liberal approach to these issues is deeply rooted in transformations in political theory that go back to the Cold War. Populism as a political rubric is seen as conforming to the coordinates of the theory of totalitarianism, as propounded most famously by Hannah Arendt. In this view, all forms of opposition to the liberal-democratic management of capitalist society, from whichever direction they come, are to be viewed as illiberal, totalitarian tendencies, and are all the more dangerous if they have mass-based roots. Society is thus only democratic to the extent that it is restricted to liberal democracy, which confines the rights and protections of individuals to those limited forms conducive to a structurally inegalitarian capitalist regime rooted in private property. Such a society, as Marxist economists Paul Baran and Paul Sweezy wrote in *Monopoly Capital*, "is democratic in form and plutocratic in content."[10] Within this dominant possessive-individualist perspective, populism has therefore come to mean all movements with any popular appeal that challenge the prevailing liberal-democratic state apparatus in advanced capitalist societies.

A major ideological shift occurred with the fall of the Soviet Union in 1991, leading to the almost universal acceptance of the liberal-democratic state as the sole bulwark against totalitarianism (and evil), a view associated in particular with Arendt. As Slavoj Žižek writes in *Did Somebody Say Totalitarianism?*:

> The elevation of Hannah Arendt into an untouchable authority . . . is perhaps the clearest sign of the theoretical defeat of the Left—of how the Left has accepted the basic coordinates of liberal democracy ("democracy" versus "totalitarianism," etc.), and is now trying to redefine its (op)position *within* this space. . . . Throughout its entire career, "totalitarianism" was an ideological notion that sustained the complex operation of "taming free radicals," of guaranteeing the liberal-democratic hegemony, dismissing the Leftist critique of liberal democracy as the obverse, the "twin," of the Rightist Fascist dictatorship. And it is useless to try to redeem 'totalitarianism' through division into subcategories (emphasizing the difference between the Fascist and Communist variety): the moment one accepts the notion of "totalitarianism," one is firmly located within the liberal-democratic horizon. The contention [here] . . . is that the notion of

> "totalitarianism," far from being an effective theoretical concept, is a kind of *stopgap*: instead of enabling us to think, forcing us to acquire a new insight into the historical reality it describes, it relieves us of the duty to think, or even actively *prevents* us from thinking.[11]

Today's conventional use of the term populism derives directly from this same "liberal-democratic horizon."[12] Populism is seen as representing incipient anti-democratic, dictatorial, and even totalitarian tendencies, to be found on both right and left, insofar as they oppose liberal democracy. Jan-Werner Müller answers the question *What Is Populism?*, raised in the title of his book, by calling populism a "danger to democracy." It can be described as "the permanent shadow of representative politics." Likewise, Cas Muddle and Cristóbal Kaltwasser state in their *Populism: A Very Short Introduction*: "Theoretically, populism is most fundamentally juxtaposed to liberal democracy." Populists are thus seen as tending toward "extremism," precisely in their opposition to the liberal-democratic state that has traditionally dominated in capitalist society.[13]

Nearly every substantive issue is lost in this definition of populism, most notably the different ways in which left and right revolts occur, their distinct class-ideological bases, and their divergent, indeed incompatible, objectives. Fascism is the antonym of liberal democracy within a capitalist society. Its advocates wish to replace liberal democracy with a different form of management of the capitalist system, removing basic civil rights and limits on executive power, strengthening the repressive apparatus to weaken working-class organization, and adopting ethno-nationalist forms of social exclusion. In contrast, socialism is the antonym, not of the liberal-democratic state, but of capitalism itself. Socialists seek to replace capitalism with an entirely different mode of production, based on both "substantive equality" and "substantive democracy."[14]

Nevertheless, faced with a resurgence of fascist tendencies in Western societies, many on the left have chosen—perhaps only for the sake of convenience—to join the Arendtian consensus. Hence, populism is portrayed even by leading analysts on the left as an incoherent and irrational attack on elites, born of anti-democratic and totalitarian tendencies. Acceptance of this view marks a significant political and ideological retreat, ceding the terms and direction of the debate to the interests of the liberal-democratic establishment.

Commenting on the hegemonic framing of the radical right as populist, and the analytical problems it presents, Andrea Mammone observes in his *Transnational Neo-Fascism in France and Italy* that "the terms populism and national populism" were deliberately introduced in recent decades by liberal European commentators in order to "replace fascism/neo-fascism as the used terminology." This move was designed to "provide a sort of political and democratic legitimization of right-wing extremism." Moreover, the rechristening of such movements as populist, Mammone argues, had less to do with any aspect of the movements themselves than with the presumption that liberal-democratic institutions were now too solid to permit an actual neo-fascist takeover. Instead, these neo-fascist forces were increasingly seen as politically malleable, with a potentially useful role in stabilizing capitalist society, checkmating the left.[15]

Likewise, political scientist Walter Laqueur notes that use of the term populist generates nothing but "great fuzziness," and requires subcategories to distinguish left from right. It is particularly misleading, he argues, with respect to the right-wing movements to which the term is most often applied. Hence, Laqueur prefers to use "neo-fascism" for what is variously called "right-wing extremism, right-wing radicalism, radical right-wing populism . . . [and] national populism"—all terms that he finds "unsatisfactory" in addressing a historically specific political tendency within the larger "fascist genus."[16]

Given this complex and contested ideological context, it is all the more important to acknowledge those notable radical commentators, including Walter Dean Burnham, Judith Butler, Noam Chomsky, Juan Cole, Henry Giroux, Paul Street, and Cornel West, who have rejected the populist designation for the Trump phenomenon and see it as part of a larger "neo-fascist wind" disrupting advanced capitalist states. Nor is this a minor issue: at stake is nothing less than the left's understanding of and response to an ascendant transnational neo-fascist movement in Europe and the United States, in the context of a deepening economic and political crisis.[17]

Political movements within the fascist genus have their mass basis in the lower-middle class or petty bourgeoisie, overlapping with the more privileged sections of the working class. The lower-middle class in the United States today comprises close to a third of the U.S. population. Its representative members are lower-level managers, semiprofessionals, craftsmen, foremen, and non-retail sales workers, with household incomes typically running around $70,000 a year.[18] It is from this stratum, and from some workers in blue-collar industries, especially in rural areas, as well as from owners of small businesses and corporate franchises, that Trump has drawn his most ardent support.[19]

In this respect, the lower-middle class can be understood as what C. Wright Mills called the "rearguarders" of the capitalist system. In times of crisis, this class often gives rise to a "radical" petty-bourgeois ideology, divorced from both more traditional working-class and liberal views: one that criticizes "crony capitalists" and government elites, while at the same time allying itself with giant corporations and the ultra-rich against an often racialized "other," namely low-income people of color, immigrants, and the working poor.[20] More privileged than the increasingly precarious majority of the working class, but denied the security and wealth of the upper-middle class, this section of the population is the one most prone to intense nationalism and racism, calling for the revival of "lost" values and traditions—or "palingenetic ultra-nationalism" (palingenesis means rebirth). Ultimately, the neo-fascist project, like classical fascism before it, relies on an alliance of the lower-middle class with monopoly-finance capital, leading ultimately to the betrayal of the movement's mass base.[21]

A "Legal Revolution"

The sheer elasticity of the concept of populism is evident in the fact that Hitler and the Nazi Party are often cited as examples of this phenomeon.[22] Classical fascism was a complex political formation that, despite the violence associated with its rise, has often been described as the result of a "legal revolution." Both Mussolini in Italy and Hitler in Germany sought to carry out their political "revolutions" within and through the capitalist state apparatus, maintaining at least a semblance of the constitutionality needed to stabilize and legitimize the new order. Indeed, the dominant image of fascism projected by the movement itself was of an "organized capitalism" under a centralized "total state"—referring to the concentration of power *within* the state—and a new, racialized vision of national sovereignty.[23]

In his legality oath at the 1930 Leipzig Reichswehr trial, Hitler told the court: "The Constitution only maps out the arena of battle, not the goal. We enter the legal agencies and in that way will make our party the determining factor. However, once we possess the constitutional power, we will mold the state into the shape we hold to be suitable." Hitler rose to power not by abolishing the Weimar Constitution, but rather, as historian Karl Bracher explained, through "the erosion and abrogation of its substance by constitutional means."[24] By November 1932, it was clear that the Nazi Party could not win a majority of the parliamentary seats. Hitler, however, would find another way to power, through his appointment as chancellor.

Once at the helm, Hitler moved quickly to invoke Article 48 of the Weimar Constitution, which authorized the executive, together with the army, to claim emergency powers and enact any measures deemed necessary to restore public order (originally intended as a safeguard against the left). This meant that the executive was free to act independently of the parliament, promulgating laws on its own, and suspending civil liberties. With the setting of the Reichstag fire at the end of February 1933, a month after he was sworn in as chancellor, Hitler was able to wield Article 48, thereby concentrating power in the executive. This was soon followed by the Enabling Act (the Law to Eliminate Peril to Nation and Reich), which further eroded the separation of powers.[25] However, the transition to full power and the consolidation of the Third Reich required a process of *Gleichschaltung*, or "bringing into line," over the course of 1933–34, during which most other branches of the state and civil society were incorporated into the new Nazi order—largely voluntarily, but under a growing terror regime.

It is important to recognize that all of this was given legal form, as was fascist management of the state in general. Historian Nikolaus Wachsmann notes that far from renouncing the law or the judiciary, the Nazi state imposed a system of "legal terror":

> The Third Reich did not become an all-out police state. Leading Nazis occasionally even made public gestures of

> support for the legal system, at least in the early years of the dictatorship. Hitler himself publicly promised in his speech on 23 March 1933 that the German judges were irremovable. At the same time, though, he also expected the legal system to fall into line with his general wishes, demanding "elasticity" in sentencing. Crucially, Hitler and other senior Nazis stressed that judges were ultimately answerable to the "national community," not to abstract legal principles. The only guideline for judges, it was said, was the welfare of the German people, and the mythical "will of the national community" was frequently invoked to justify brutal punishment. That this "will" was in reality nothing more than the will of the Nazi leaders, or more precisely Hitler's own, was not seen as a contradiction. . . . The legal apparatus was an essential element of Nazi terror. It played a central role in the criminalisation of political dissent and the politicisation of common crime. Trials were not completely hidden from the public. On the contrary, the Nazi media were full of news about court cases and sentences.[26]

Hitler explicitly refused to set aside the Weimar Constitution and codify his new order, arguing that "justice is a means of ruling. Justice is the codified practice of ruling." A new constitution would therefore be premature, and would only weaken the "revolution." Eventually, of course, the *Gleichschaltung* process was complete, and the identification of the Führer with the law was absolute. Under the resulting *Führerprinzip*, as the Nazi jurist Carl Schmitt wrote, "the Führer safeguards the Reich."[27]

Similarly, Mussolini's defenders always insisted, in the words of Italian fascist Julius Evola, that *Il Duce* "did not 'seize' power, but received it from the King, and under the conformist institutional garb of entrusting the government to him there was the equivalent of a sort of completely legal investiture."[28] Fascist propaganda strained to give to Mussolini's dictatorship the trappings of constitutionalism, as if the October 1922 March on Rome had never taken place. This appearance of legality was only made possible by the support of the capitalist class and the military, as well as the broader political right. The elaborate performance of constitutional order continued even as systematic repression and authoritarianism deepened.

A defining feature of fascism was its continuation of the capitalist separation of state and economy, even as the role of the state was transformed. The very notion of the "privatization" of the economy, now associated with neoliberalism, was a Nazi invention, reflecting the Third Reich's massive denationalization of industry in sectors such as steel, mining, shipbuilding, and banking.[29] Command of industry and finance was returned to capital. The Nazi state strongly favored economic concentration, passing legislation designed to promote cartels. Tax policy likewise favored the capitalist class: "Tax increases were levied primarily upon non-business taxpayers in the population. The tax burden was thus enlarged for wage earners and consumer groups in general."[30] And though Hitler's concern to protect big business and private property did not prevent him from encouraging embezzlement and corruption among his associates, in general private property (at least for "racially pure" Germans) and the institutions of capitalism remained sacrosanct.[31]

At the same time, fascist regimes in both Italy and Germany were known for supporting and even expanding the welfare state, albeit with racial exclusions. Social provision grew enormously under Mussolini, garnering global praise. In Germany, the welfare state was a cornerstone of the regime. As historian Sheri Berman writes: "The Nazis . . . supported an extensive welfare state (of course, for 'ethnically pure' Germans). It included free higher education, family and child support, pensions, health insurance, and an array of publicly supported entertainment and vacation options." Economic expansion, driven by demand generated through spending on infrastructure and the military, ensured full employment, even as unions were abolished and wages repressed. The number of unemployed fell from almost 6 million in 1933, when Hitler came to power, to 2.4 million at the end of 1934, when he was to consolidate his power as Führer. By 1938, Germany had effectively achieved full employment, while most other capitalist countries were still mired in the Great Depression (the unemployment rate in the United States that year was 19 percent). In the eyes of much of the world, fascism's claim to legitimacy was that it had found a way to make capitalism work, even as it appeared to be disintegrating elsewhere.[32]

None of this is to deny the deeply repressive character of the fascist state, its abrogation of human rights, its militarism, imperialism, and racism.[33] Yet, at the same time the classical fascist state sought to legitimate itself and consolidate its position with the population—or that part of the population that it considered its mass base. Once in power, however, fascist states purged many of their more "radical" followers (as in the "Night of the Long Knives," June 30 to July 2, 1934, in Hitler's Germany) in the process of linking up more firmly with monopoly capital.

Today's neo-fascism builds on these earlier fascist myths of the "legal revolution," along with the notion of a more organized, efficient capitalist state, able to transcend the liberal-democratic impasse. It promises both policies of ethno-national exclusion and of revitalized economic growth and employment through infrastructure spending and military expansion. At the same time, it is often less inclined than the traditional right to attack the welfare state or to promote austerity. In France, Marine Le Pen's National Front has recently tried to remake itself as a more broadly "anti-establishment" party, exploiting popular discontent to attract a wider range of supporters, including some who formerly identified with the left. Despite this cynical rebranding, the party's politics of petty-bourgeois resentment, reactionary Catholicism, and virulent xenophobia, together with its link to the upper echelons of the capitalist class, mark it as neo-fascist.[34]

Like the classical fascism of Italy and Germany in the 1920s and '30s, neo-fascism arises from interrelated crises of capitalism and the liberal-democratic state, undermining the latter while seeking to shore up the former. Given that explicit identification with classical fascism remains taboo in mainstream politics, organized neo-fascism today is presented as formally democratic and populist, adhering to legal-constitutional structures. Nevertheless, like all movements in the fascist genus, neo-fascist ideology combines racist, nationalist, and culturalist myths with economic and political proposals aimed primarily at the lower-middle class (or petty bourgeoisie) in alliance with monopoly capital—while also seeking to integrate nationalistic working-class supporters and rural populations. Increasingly, neo-fascism draws support from relatively privileged wage workers that in the late twentieth century enjoyed a degree of prosperity and status but who now find their living conditions imperiled in the stagnating advanced capitalist economy of the early twenty-first century.[35]

The single most important ideological figure in the growth of neo-fascism in Europe in the post–Second World War years, and in the promotion of its distinct cultural perspective, was the Italian philosopher Julius Evola (1898–1974). As Laqueur has observed, Evola was at the "extreme wing of historical fascism," influencing Mussolini with respect to race and racism, and later turning to Hitler as a more authentic representative of the fascist project. Significantly, Evola was present at Hitler's general headquarters in 1943 on the very day when the Waffen-SS troops were to bring Mussolini there, following their rescue of him from imprisonment in Italy after he was deposed. In the 1930s, Evola wrote: "Everything that is heroism and the dignity of the warrior in our conception must be considered justified from a higher point of view: in the same way that we have to oppose, with complete precision and on all levels, everything that is a democratic and levelling disorder."[36] Evola was known for his virulent anti-Semitism, even by the standards of the time. He frequently criticized fascism for not being pure enough.

Following the Second World War, Evola was to develop a set of neo-fascist theoretical works under the mantle of "traditionalism," including postwar editions of his fascist treatise *Revolt Against the Modern World* (1934), as well as such works as *Men Among the Ruins* (1953), *Ride the Tiger* (1961), *The Path of Cinnabar* (1963), and *Fascism Viewed from the Right* (1970). The fascism of Italy and Germany in the 1920s and 1930s, he argued, needed to be defended in its "positive" aspects and separated from the specific mistakes that Hitler and Mussolini made that led to its defeat in the Second World War. As Evola scholar H. T. Hansen put it in his Introduction to *Men Among the Ruins*, Evola came to be viewed as "the 'spiritual father' of a group of radical 'neo-fascists' (in the broad sense of the word)." Giorgio Almirante, party chairman of the MSI (Movimento Sociale Italiano), heir to the old Fascist Party, called Evola "the Marcuse of the Right, only better."[37]

Evola's cultural analysis emphasized the values of tradition, spiritualism, idealism, hierarchy, and counterrevolution, and pointed to the need for a new "warrior" class.[38] He wrote in

Ride the Tiger: When material incentives do not suffice, "the only influence over the masses today—and now even more than ever—is on the plane of impassioned and subintellectual forces, which by their very nature lack any stability. These are the forces that demagogues, popular leaders, manipulators of myths, and fabricators of 'public opinion' count on. In this regard, we can learn from yesterday's regimes in Germany and Italy that positioned themselves against democracy and Marxism."[39] The pure-fascist or neo-fascist state would be organized around superior, elite racial stocks, divesting itself of "inferior races." Aryanism needed to be interpreted not as related simply to the Germanic stock, but in a way that encompassed Europeans more broadly, or at least the "Aryan-Roman" race.[40] Evola also wrote of the "decadence of modern woman" and the "feminist idiocy." The revolt against the modern world included a revolt against science. "None of modern science," he stated, "has the slightest value as knowledge."[41]

Although Evola had no economic analysis to speak of, he insisted that the state of the new fascist era, like that of the old, should be based on private property and corporatism, with the destruction of any autonomous working-class organizations. The state, though, should retain its relative autonomy, securing the entire system from above, through its monopoly of the use of force. Sovereignty, viewed in palingenetic, ultra-nationalistic, and authoritarian terms, needed to be "absolute."[42]

Evola and other neo-fascist thinkers, such as the influential French theorist Alain de Benoist, created the ideological foundations for the transnational neo-fascist movement that emerged in Europe in the 1970s and later spread to the United States. The movement was to gain a mass following as a result of the increasing economic stagnation in the advanced capitalist world, and it has grown by leaps and bounds since the Great Financial Crisis of 2007–2009. Nevertheless, the organizational roots of many of these developments were formed in Europe in the 1970s. This can be seen, for example, in the formation of what were called "Hobbit Camps" for neo-fascist youth in Italy (named after the creatures in J. R. R. Tolkien's novels), with the notion of Hobbits standing for the lower-middle class, the largely forgotten population rising up to transform the world. This same idea was later to catch on with the alt-right in the United States.[43] A key figure today in what Mammone calls the "transnational neo-fascist movement" is the Russian philosopher Aleksandr Dugin, who has built his "fourth political theory" on Evola's ideas (as well as on those of Schmitt, de Benoist, and the German philosopher Martin Heidegger), attracting the favorable attention of the U.S. alt-right.[44]

Trump and the Neo-Fascist Alliance

Ironically, it is in the United States, where there are no neo-fascist parties of any electoral standing, that the "radical right" has enjoyed its greatest victory so far. From the Republican primaries to his defeat of Hillary Clinton in the Electoral College, Trump's path to the White House depended on his appeal to the lower-middle class and parts of the white working class, as well as rural and evangelical Christian voters. At every turn, Trump's campaign flouted convention and propriety, instead exploiting Evola's "impassioned and subintellectual forces."

A key source of Trump's success was his connection to the alt-right, in particular Breitbart News and its CEO, Steve Bannon, who became Trump's campaign manager. Channeling the radical right's contempt for the political establishment, the Bannon-Breitbart strategy spoke to the fears and resentments of a decisive section of the lower-middle and working classes. With Bannon's help, Trump also attracted the strategic support of certain powerful members of the capitalist class, particularly the Silicon Valley tycoon Peter Thiel and the billionaire hedge fund mogul Robert Mercer and his daughter Rebekah.[45] Trump's quintessentially neo-fascist strategy of enlisting mass support through racist and nativist appeals to lower-middle class insecurities, while allying with core elements of the ruling class, has sown confusion in elite political circles and the corporate media. Lacking any historical or class references, mainstream pundits saw his campaign as a confused hybrid of right and left. Some otherwise astute analysts on the left portrayed him as a "centrist," while still others insisted that he had no principles or plan at all, that his chaotic campaign was governed only by the candidate's egoistic impulses.[46]

Nevertheless, what should be clear at this point is that the Trump administration came into office with what can only be called a neo-fascist political project. Trump's domestic agenda reflected the class alliances and "subintellectual" ideology that brought him to power. In addition to the well-known "Muslim ban" and the proposed wall along the U.S.-Mexico border, the Trump administration has pressed for "deconstruction of the administrative state" (as Bannon called it); the gutting of the environmental protection and scientific agencies; the elimination of most federal regulations on business; a trillion-dollar increase in infrastructure spending; privatization of education; a huge rise in military spending; the effective elimination of Obamacare; the end of net neutrality; and steep cuts to taxes on corporations and the rich. Trump has filled his cabinet and advisory positions with a ghoulish ensemble of billionaires, Wall Street insiders, hardline generals, alt-right ideologues, and climate-change deniers.[47]

Although it is true that the administration's early months were marked by fierce battles inside the West Wing between alt-right true believers and more "moderate" plutocratic interests, these conflicts only reflected the inherent contradictions in the neo-fascist alliance that has thus far defined the Trump White House. The representatives of the alt-right are preoccupied with pure power politics and with bringing the federal branches and bureaucracies into line, while the plutocrats—Trump's real constituency—appear to be steering the administration toward a newly unfettered form of corporate oligarchy.[48]

The symbolic rivals in this factional struggle are Bannon, the alt-right firebreather who stands for Trump's base—though he is himself an alumnus of Goldman Sachs and a consummate elite insider—and Trump's son-in-law and adviser, Jared Kushner, a real estate scion seeking to safeguard the interests of financial capital. Bannon, though supporting a hard-nosed capitalism, is primarily concerned with deconstructing the administrative state and producing political results that appeal to Trump's base. The key to winning an election, he explains, is "to play to people without a college education. High school people. That's how you win elections." His main interest is thus in carrying out a "political revolution."[49] Kushner, in contrast, is a more politically detached figure, concerned first and foremost with questions of capital accumulation and furthering the interests of the ruling class—thus representing Trump's own ultimate interest. At present, the administration's focus seems to be on loosening all restraints on corporate cronyism and instituting tax reform in favor of the plutocrats: Kushner's domain. But as the midterm elections near, Trump will likely swing back toward the alt-right, at least rhetorically, Bannon's domain.

In the imperial sphere, the administration, as we have seen, initially sought a détente with Russia, with the object of shifting the full force of the U.S. empire against the Islamic world (or that part of it in the Middle East and Africa not securely within the U.S. empire) and China. This planned geopolitical shift put the White House at odds with both the national security "deep state" and leading sections of the capitalist class, and only heightened the conflict between the Kushner and Bannon factions within the White House. But with his first national security advisor, Michael Flynn, forced to resign over his alleged ties to Russia, and with his poll numbers at historic lows, Trump abruptly changed course by launching an attack on Syria. In one stroke, Trump donned the attire of commander-in-chief, to near-universal media acclaim: in the words of CNN pundit Fareed Zakaria, he "became president of the United States" that night.

Thus, within little more than two weeks from late March to mid-April, the world witnessed dramatically increased civilian casualties from U.S. bombings in the Middle East, as Trump turned day-to-day decisions over to the military commanders on the ground. This was accompanied by Trump's launching of fifty-nine cruise missiles at a Syrian air base; the dropping of "the mother of all bombs" in Afghanistan; and explicit threats of military action against North Korea.[50]

Some commentators naïvely suggested that this pivot toward a war-room posture on the part of the administration conflicted with its supposed original "isolationist" values and therefore represented a shift to the center. The mainstream media went so far as to declare that Trump's reversals (including the removal of Bannon from the National Security Council) meant that he had finally decided on a more "presidential" course. In fact, these were precisely the kind of violent swings in U.S. imperial posture that were to be expected from a neo-fascist White House. The original détente with Russia was dropped, without the abandonment of any of the new administration's earlier geopolitical objectives, aimed at increasing pressure on the Islamic State and China.[51]

The stark reality is that under Trump, the United States is being armed to the teeth, and is exhibiting greater signs of belligerence. The new administration has now signed on to the neoconservative strategy of simultaneously opposing both Russia and China. Nor should this be occasion for any particular surprise. Significantly, it was none other than Bannon who declared: "America has to be strong—economically strong and militarily strong. And a strong America could be ultimately a provider of Pax Americana," that is, a new unipolar world empire. None of this places Trump outside the mainstream of U.S. foreign policy. Indeed, the demand to restore U.S. power abroad is supported by the entire U.S. ruling class, as evidenced by Hillary Clinton's promise on the campaign trail to impose no-fly zones in Syria, which would have brought the world to the brink of a global thermonuclear war, and by her strong support of Trump's actions against Syria. Nevertheless, the Trump administration in its short time in office has managed to signal a bravado and recklessness in the use of force, coupled with a shift toward military over civilian control in this area, that is nothing short of ominous.[52]

The New Barbarism

As indicated above, the White House has been the site of competing allegiances: responses to the interests of monopoly-finance capital on one side, and to Trump's lower-middle-class base on the other. Though there is no doubt that the administration will ultimately prioritize the former over the latter, betraying its claims to populism, to retain any credibility with its base the White House nonetheless must perform an elaborate dance. It must promote the interests of the corporate rich, while distancing itself from the upper-middle-class professional strata so loathed by Trump's supporters.[53]

His policies must give "expression" to lower-middle-class interests and, to some extent, working-class demands, even if these are not to be realized.[54] The political and strategic constellation represented by Bannon, Breitbart, and the Mercers is therefore vital.

Hence, the neo-fascist strategy that marks the Trump White House thus far is likely to continue, incorporating both the alt-right and plutocratic factions. Upon entering the White House, Trump immediately raised up representatives of the alt-right, who had been key to his campaign. Here the role of Bannon, still Trump's chief strategist, and the main link to Breitbart, remains central. Ideologically the alt-right relies on the ideas of thinkers such as Evola, Dugin, and Oswald Spengler (the influential early twentieth-century German historian and author of *The Decline of the West*).[55] Bannon has demonstrated considerable acquaintance with Evola's work, professing admiration for Evola's "traditionalism . . . particularly the sense of where it supports the underpinnings of nationalism" and the expansion of white-European cultural sovereignty. For Bannon, the right's global struggle is to be seen in terms of a renewal of the historic war of the "Judeo-Christian West" against Islam, now extended to include the national-cultural exclusion of non-white immigrants into Europe and the United States.[56]

A crucial part of the streamlined neo-fascist appeal that Bannon imparted early on to the Trump campaign and then carried over to the White House is geared to economic nationalism. Bannon argues that "the globalists gutted the American working class and created a middle class in Asia." This points to a kind of empire in reverse, where working-class, white Americans, who formerly benefitted from unrivaled U.S. hegemony in the world economy, are now seeing their jobs taken away by Asians, while they are being flooded by "illegal" Latino immigrants, and by refugees from Middle East countries dominated by "radical Islamic terrorists." Crony capitalists, financiers on the take, and liberal globalists are all to blame. Trump, Bannon, Breitbart, and the alt-right rely heavily on racially coded language (or dog whistles) as signals to reach their more militant white supporters, who are encouraged to see immigrants, refugees, and non-white populations generally as constituting a combined economic and cultural threat.[57]

The racial strategy can be seen in Bannon's repeated references metaphorically to *The Camp of the Saints*. This is the title of a novel by French writer Jean Raspail; undoubtedly one of the most racist works of its kind ever published. In 1975, when the book was translated into English, the usually staid *Kirkus Reviews* wrote that "the publishers are presenting *The Camp of the Saints* as a major event, and it probably is, in much the same sense that *Mein Kampf* was a major event." This rabidly racist novel depicts an invasion by 800,000 "wretched creatures," refugees in the derelict Last Chance Armada, who seek to take over France as a beachhead into white Europe, "the camp of the saints." Meanwhile hordes of Chinese threaten Russia, a French cruise ship has been seized in Manila, and barricades have been erected by whites around black ghettos in New York. The title comes from the Book of Revelation (20:9): "And they went up on the breadth of the earth, and compassed the camp of the saints about, and the beloved city: and fire came down from the God of heaven, and devoured them." From page 1 on, *The Camp of the Saints* is full of murder, rape, carnage, atrocities, and the most extreme forms of racism, reducing people to body parts, with severed (racially signified) body parts strewn everywhere. Its cover advertises it as "the apocalyptic, controversial, bestselling novel about the end of the white world." It is intended to generate the emotional, subintellectual basis, in Evola's terms, for unutterable violence, directed not just at Asians but at all non-white races, who are seen as racial threats.[58]

The Camp of the Saints has been taken up by the alt-right as a kind of racist code. For Bannon, it refers to refugees flooding from the Middle East and Africa into Europe. As he declared in 2015, "It's been almost a Camp of the Saints-type invasion into Central and then Western and Northern Europe." A year later, he stated, "The whole thing in Europe is all about immigration. It's a global issue today—this kind of global Camp of the Saints." About the same time, he said, "It's not a migration. It's really an invasion. I call it the Camp of the Saints."[59] After pointedly alluding to *The Camp of the Saints* in an interview with Jeff Sessions—now U.S. Attorney General, whom Bannon has described as "one of the intellectual, moral leaders of this populist, nationalist movement in this country"—Bannon asked, "Do you believe the elites in this country have the backbone, have the belief in the underlying principles of the Judeo-Christian West to actually win this war [against immigrants, refugees and Islam]?" Sessions answered, "I'm worried about that."[60] Others have taken this up as well. Iowa GOP Congressman Steve King, referred in a radio interview in March 2017 to the possibility of race wars in the United States today, strongly recommending that people read *The Camp of Saints* in this context.[61]

Trumpism is rife on a daily basis with racism, misogyny, and extreme nationalism. Bannon and Breitbart refer coyly to the alt-right movement as one made up of "working-class Hobbits," a term for its "forgotten" white, lower-middle-class/working-class adherents. This refers back to a negative reference by Arizona Republican Senator John McCain to Tea Party "Hobbits."[62] Bannon took it up as an ironic term, standing for Trump's hardcore constituency. In doing so, though, he was undoubtedly aware of the earlier neo-fascist "Hobbit camps" that had been formed in Italy, with a similar meaning. Indeed, the U.S. alt-right, as represented by Breitbart, could be described today as a toxic mixture of European neo-fascism, U.S. white supremacism, and Christian fundamentalism.

The Trump phenomenon draws on some of the most sordid aspects of the U.S. past, including genocide (of Native Americans), slavery, Jim Crow, and imperialism. Of all U.S. presidents, the one that is seen by Bannon (and by Trump himself) as most closely related to the new resident at 1600 Pennsylvania Avenue is Andrew Jackson. This is ostensibly because of the popular-democratic upsurge associated with him and his attack on the Bank of the United States; but also undoubtedly because of his wealthy slaveholder status, his gruesome role in the Indian Wars, and his government's forcible removal of the southeastern tribes in the Trail of Tears. Trump declared in an interview in April 2017 that if Jackson had still been alive (he died sixteen years before the Confederate forces opened fire on Fort Sumter) and presumably had he been president, he would have prevented the Civil War—an absurd statement doubtless meant as a dog whistle to Trump's alt-right, white supremacist supporters, who idealize the slave South and the Confederacy.[63]

Trump's own outlook and ambitions intersect ideologically with the alt-right as his 2011 book, *Tough Times: Make America Great Again*, shows. Trump declared on the campaign trail that "the only important thing is the unification of the people—because the other people don't mean anything."[64] Nevertheless, the owner of Trump Tower in Manhattan represents monopoly-finance capital, first and foremost. Indeed, Trump's attacks on "crony capitalism" and his calls for "draining the swamp" are belied by the billionaires and lobbyists that he has brought into his administration, and the cronyism that is everywhere visible, starting with his own family and extending to the special access to the president for those ultra-wealthy interests who belong to his Mar-a-Lago Golf Club.[65]

The neo-fascist thrust of the Trump White House can be seen in those chosen to occupy key strategic roles. An example of this is Curtis Ellis, a member of Trump's beachhead transition team, appointed as special assistant to the Secretary of Labor. Ellis, a Breitbart author, wrote an article in May 2016 for the *World News Daily* called "The Radical Left's Ethnic Cleansing of America." In this article, which was to be celebrated by Bannon and featured on Breitbart, Ellis argued that, for the globalist left, "the death (literally) of white working people is a desired outcome, a feature not a bug. . . . The death of American working-class whites was planned by the radical left and carried out with willing executioners at the highest levels of American politics, academia and business."[66] Such nationalistic-racist views aimed at the left and at non-white populations were strongly encouraged by Trump in his campaign for the presidency, and in his actions since coming into office.

Trumponomics and the Crisis of the U.S. Political Economy

"The neoliberal era in the United States," Cornel West declared, "ended with a neo-fascist bang."[67] Neoliberalism was itself a ruling-class response to the deepening economic stagnation of the capitalist economy, as the quarter-century of prosperity from the late 1940s through the early 1970s broke down. Needing a stimulus in the Reagan period, the U.S. economy resorted first to military spending and tax cuts, but soon benefitted more fundamentally from the long decline in interest rates (the so-called Greenspan put), which fed a period of vast debt-credit expansion and what Paul Sweezy called "the financialization of the capital accumulation process."[68] The result was a bubble economy that continued into the Clinton and George W. Bush presidencies, and then came to a sudden end with the bursting of the housing bubble and the subsequent crisis of 2007–2009. Trillions of dollars were poured into corporate coffers in an attempt to "bail out" defaulting financial institutions, as well as heavily indebted non-financial corporations. The subsequent economic recovery, as noted previously, has been one of sluggish growth or secular stagnation—a period of "endless crisis."[69]

Everywhere neoliberalism has come to stand for policies of austerity, financial speculation, globalization, income polarization, and corporate cronyism, creating what Michael Yates has called "The Great Inequality."[70] "Across the advanced economies," Michael Jacobs and Mariana Mazzucato write, "the share of GDP going to labor fell by 9 percent on average between 1980 and 2007. . . . In the United States, between 1975 and 2012, the top 1 percent gained around 47 percent of the total increase in incomes."[71] Wealth inequality has increased even faster. In 1963, the average wealth of families in the ninety-ninth percentile in the United States was six times that of wealth holders in the fiftieth percentile; in 2013, it was twelve times.[72]

All of this has been accompanied by the erosion of U.S. hegemony in the world economy; the growth of a new imperialism based on the global labor arbitrage (taking advantage of wage differentials between the Global North and South); the changing role of manufacturing and investment in the context of the digital revolution; and neoliberal attacks on labor. These factors have enormously undermined the position of the working population in the United States, while also intensifying the exploitation of workers in the Global South. What was once seen—in hyped-up fashion—as a "social contract" between capital and labor in the heyday of

U.S. hegemony and prosperity has now disintegrated entirely. With it has disappeared what was once called the "labor aristocracy," a minority of relatively privileged, largely unionized workers in the advanced capitalist world who benefitted indirectly from unrivaled U.S. imperial hegemony and the siphoning of profits from the Global South.[73] Monopoly-finance capital now freely outsources production from the Global North to the Global South, in what has become a new age of imperialism characterized by a race to the bottom for workers throughout the world economy.[74]

The social democratic campaign of Bernie Sanders in the 2016 election showed the potential for a grassroots left upsurge in this context—the main fear of the ruling class. But Sanders's extraordinary campaign, representing an approach that would undoubtedly have won in a contest with Trump by drawing on a far wider working-class base, was blocked by a Democratic Party establishment that had long since put into place a superdelegate system and a structure of control through the Democratic National Committee, expressly designed to prevent such a left-liberal or social democratic takeover of the party. The road was thus left open to Trump. In this context there is no real doubt about the source of Trump's success. He received a remarkable 77 percent of the vote among those who said their financial situation had worsened in the preceding four years.[75]

Few understood this overall economic dynamic better that Bannon, the strategic brains behind the Trump campaign, who had worked on Wall Street as an investment banker—before moving to Hollywood and making ultra-right-wing political films, testing the zeitgeist, and finally taking over Breitbart. With a realism completely lacking in neoliberal circles, he remarked, "I don't think there's any doubt that the world is in the beginning state of a crisis that it can't avoid." Raging against liberals, he stated that the left globalists destroyed "the American working class. . . . The issue now is about Americans looking to not get f—ed over."[76]

Trump's declarations about the "carnage" in the U.S. economy in his Inaugural Address (written by Bannon and his Breitbart colleague Stephen Miller, now a special adviser to Trump); his claims that the United States should have taken the Iraqi oil as payment for its deposing Saddam Hussein; and his self-styled "truthful hyperbole" regarding labor statistics (he claimed the unemployment rate in 2016 was "as high as 35 [percent]" or more) were all part of this same strategy.[77] This also included his attack on unfair trade (taken from the playbook of the left), his emphasis on protecting Social Security, his proposal to cut prescription drug prices through competitive bidding, and his promised trillion dollars for infrastructure spending. All of this was designed to draw support from wage workers that the Democrats had abandoned.

Likewise, the virulent attacks on illegal immigrants and refugees, the building of the wall between the United States and Mexico, and Trump's strong law-and-order stance (including suggestions that Black Lives Matter be put under federal surveillance) were all part of the attempt to consolidate mass support for Trump *in class-economic and racial terms.*[78]

Casting aside the Obama-era Trans-Pacific Partnership, Trump has raised the prospect of trade and currency wars with China to save American jobs. He appointed as director of the White House National Trade Council economist Peter Navarro, author of *The Coming China Wars*, which accuses China of currency manipulation and unleashing a "new imperialism" on the globe. The United States, Navarro argues, should end its "mutually parasitic economic codependence" with China and fight back economically (and militarily). Among Navarro's other works are *Death by China*

(2011) and *Crouching China: What China's Militarism Means to the World* (2015).[79]

Trump has vowed to more than double the rate of growth of the economy. Yet his economic policy is largely a supply-side fantasy, which proclaims that rapid growth will automatically follow the gigantic windfalls to monopoly-finance capital resulting from wholesale deregulation, and from lavish tax cuts for the wealthy and the corporations they own. He repeatedly declared that he would hugely expand infrastructure spending, which would give a boost to the real estate and construction sectors. But since the Trump plan is based on tax cuts to firms, thus payng them to do what they would likely have done anyway, rather than a massive increase in spending, and is supposed to be strung out over ten years, it will do little to stimulate the economy as a whole. Indeed, none of this can lift the economy out of stagnation. The most likely result is continued slow growth, possibly interrupted by a bubble effect in the financial sector.[80] The one thing that is certain is the business cycle. The economy is nearing its peak and recession is on the horizon, expected by many economists to commence within a few years.

Any prospect for real economic gains for the mass of the population will run into the triple contradiction of economic stagnation, financial crisis, and declining U.S. hegemony that characterize the epoch of monopoly-finance capital. Rather than alter these conditions, Trump's economic policy is likely to aggravate them. This means that the Trump regime will, as its only economic option, probably gravitate to further military spending increases and imperialist adventures, coupled with greater economic repression of workers at home, particularly among the poorest sectors of the workforce—conceived as the surest way to "Make America Great Again."

The greatest danger under these circumstances is that an increase in internal repression—Bannon is on record as supporting Joseph McCarthy's anti-Communist witch hunt in the 1950s—will have as its counterpart an increase in external repression and war without bounds, seen as a way of spurring the economy.[81] Certain restraints on the global use of force have already been removed. A new upsurge in barbarism nationally and internationally is in the wind, this time armed with weapons capable of destroying the world as a place for human habitation. Indeed, the exterminism that is a real danger in these circumstances is already evident in the renunciation of all efforts to contain climate change, which Trump calls a "hoax." This, then, threatens the eventual collapse of civilization (and even the extinction of humanity) under a continuation of capitalist business as usual.

Resistance in the "Post-Truth Society"

In "Writing the Truth: Five Difficulties" Brecht stated:

> Nowadays, anyone who wishes to combat lies and ignorance and to write the truth must overcome at least five difficulties. He must have the *courage* to write the truth when truth is everywhere opposed; the *keenness* to recognize it, although it is everywhere concealed; the *skill* to manipulate it as a weapon; the *judgment* to select those in whose hands it will be effective; and the *cunning* to spread the truth among such persons. These are formidable problems for writers living under Fascism, but they exist also for those writers who have fled or been exiled; they exist even for writers in countries where civil liberty prevails.[82]

Brecht would not be at all surprised that the rapid growth of neo-fascism in the United States and Europe has coincided with the declaration by the Oxford Dictionaries that the "word of the year" for 2016—in recognition of Trump's political rise—was the adjective "post-truth." Significantly, another word on the short list for word of the year was "alt-right." The Oxford Dictionaries define "post-truth" as "relating to or denoting circumstances in which objective facts are less influential in shaping public opinion than appeals to emotion and personal belief."[83]

Blatant violation of the truth, and what Georg Lukács called "the destruction of reason," has always been associated with fascism, and has helped prepare the ground for its rise.[84] It is impossible to understand our current social reality divorced from class analysis; nor is it possible to resist that reality effectively without class organization. A defining feature of contemporary liberal-democratic ideology, which set the conditions for today's post-truth society, has been "the retreat from class," and particularly from the notion of the working class—ironically brought back into the mainstream in relation to Trump.[85] This makes it possible for the vague term "populism" to cloak the growing neo-fascist threat of our time.

Resistance to these trends is only possible, as Brecht reminds us, by first having the courage, the keenness, the skill, the judgment, and the cunning to address the truth with respect to this demonic political phenomenon. It is necessary to recognize the truth in its historical, structural, and dialectical connections, insisting on the fact that today's neo-fascism is the inevitable product of the crisis of monopoly-finance capital. Hence, the only effective way to resist is to resist the system itself. Against today's "neo-fascist wind," the movement toward socialism is the final barricade, the only genuine class-human-ecological defense.

Trump and Climate Catastrophe

> This very expensive GLOBAL WARMING bullshit has got to stop. Our planet is freezing, record low temps, and our GW scientists are stuck in ice.
>
> —DONALD TRUMP, JANUARY 2, 2014[1]

The alarm bells are ringing. The climate-change denialism of the Trump administration, coupled with its goal of maximizing fossil-fuel extraction and consumption at all costs, constitutes, in the words of Noam Chomsky, "almost a death knell for the human species." As noted climatologist Michael E. Mann has declared, "I fear that this may be game over for the climate."[2]

The effects of the failure to mitigate global warming will not, of course, come all at once, and will not affect all regions and populations equally. But just a few years of inaction in the immediate future could lock in dangerous climate change that would be irreversible for the next ten thousand years.[3] It is feared that once the climatic point of no return—usually seen as a 2°C increase in global average temperatures—is reached, positive-feedback mechanisms will set in, accelerating warming trends and leading, in the words of James Hansen, former director of NASA's Goddard Institute for Space Studies and the foremost U.S. climate scientist, to "a dynamic situation that is out of [human] control," propelling the world toward the 4°C (or even higher) future that is thought by scientists to portend the end of civilization, in the sense of organized human society.[4]

Although the United States currently contributes only about 15 percent of global carbon-dioxide emissions, a failure on its part to act to reduce emissions would push the world more decisively toward the 2°C tipping point.[5] Moreover, in the event that the principal per-capita global emitter and the hegemonic global power chooses to bow out, any worldwide effort to reduce carbon emissions will be severely jeopardized. For this reason, climate scientists are increasingly turning from the United States to China as the main hope for leadership in combatting climate change.[6]

At this critical moment in history, three questions need to be answered: What does the latest scientific evidence tell us about the approach of climate catastrophe? How is today's monopoly-finance capitalism, with Donald Trump as its authentic representative, contributing to this impending planetary catastrophe? And what possibilities remain for humanity to avert an Earth System calamity?

Toward a "Fatal Imbalance"

The latest evidence on climate change is jaw-dropping. On November 8, 2016, the day of the U.S. election, the World Meteorological Organization reported that global average temperatures have risen to about 1.2°C above preindustrial levels (dangerously close to the initial 1.5°C boundary set by the 2015 Paris Climate Agreement), with 2016 the hottest year on record, surpassing 2015 and 2014, both of which were themselves record-breaking years.[7]

The annual *Arctic Report Card* of the National Oceanic and Atmospheric Administration, released in December 2016, showed that Arctic temperatures are rising at rates twice the global average, with an average annual increase over land areas of 3.5°C since the beginning of the twentieth century. Arctic sea ice is critical for climate stability because of the "albedo effect," in which white ice reflects the sun's rays. The disappearance of sea ice and its replacement with a heat-absorbing "dark ocean" thus represents a major positive climate feedback. In September 2016, Arctic sea ice dropped to its second-lowest level ever recorded. The Greenland ice sheet, meanwhile, continues its rapid loss of mass, further contributing to sea level rise. The *Arctic Resilience Report*, published in November 2016 by the Stockholm Environment Institute, emphasized that Arctic temperatures had peaked at around 20°C warmer than normal for that time of year, and warned of nineteen impending tipping points affecting the stability of the Arctic region, some of which could "tip" the entire global climate, including much higher releases of methane—a far more potent greenhouse gas than carbon dioxide—due to the thawing of the tundra.[8]

Over the last two years, the scientific community has nearly doubled its projections for sea level rise during the course of this century. It has already increased about 8 inches, threatening island communities and low-lying coastal areas throughout the world. The ocean could rise by close to two meters (more than six feet) by 2100, and, over a couple of centuries, the increase could reach six meters (twenty feet). By 2500, according to one study in *Nature*, sea level rise could be as much as 15 meters (over 49 feet).[9]

Trillionthtonne.org, a climate-tracking website associated with scientists at the University of Oxford, currently indicates that if present trends continue unchecked, the world will hit the trillionth-metric-ton mark in total carbon emissions—that is, the amount of total carbon emissions thought to generate 450 ppm in global carbon concentration and a 2°C increase in global temperatures—in just over twenty years. Over 600 gigatons (billions of metric tons) of carbon have been emitted into the atmosphere so far. The closer the world gets to the trillionth metric ton, the more drastic the effort needed to avoid breaking the planetary carbon budget. At present, this would require planet-wide carbon-emissions reductions of around 3 percent a year, and as much as three times that number in rich, high per-capita carbon-emitting nations, which account for more than a quarter of the world's present emissions as well as the vast majority of its historic emissions—and whose wealth offers them ample material means to address the problem.[10]

As Mann, best known for developing the famous "hockey-stick" chart showing the sharp rise in global average temperatures, concisely explains in his 2016 book *The Madhouse Effect*:

> A tipping point is, of course, a point of no return. In the context of climate change, it would mean that we have warmed the planet enough to set in motion an unstoppable process. In reality, there is no single tipping point in the climate system; there are many. And the farther we go down the fossil fuel highway, the more tipping points we will cross. Many observers have argued that a warming of the planet of 3.6°F (2°C) relative to preindustrial levels (something that will likely happen if we allow CO_2 levels to climb to just 450 ppm) would almost certainly create dangerous, potentially irreversible changes in our climate. As a reminder, we have already warmed around 1.5°F (1°C), and another 0.9°F (0.5°C) is likely in the pipeline. Another decade of business-as-usual fossil fuel emissions could commit us to that 3.6°F (2°C) "dangerous warming" threshold. . . .
>
> At the current rate of 30 gigatons a year, we'll burn through our [carbon] budget in about three decades. To remain within the budget, we have to reduce emissions

> by several percent a year, to bring them down to 33 percent of current levels within twenty years. That's an average worldwide carbon footprint similar to what prevails in the developing world. By midcentury, emissions must approach zero. *That's* the black double-diamond slope.
>
> One recent analysis determined that achieving these reductions would require that 33 percent of all proven reserves of oil, 50 percent of all natural gas, and 80 percent of all coal reserves must remain in the ground. That means we have to phase out coal and leave most if not all of the Canadian tar sands in the ground (that is, no Keystone XL pipeline).[11]

The issue before us, as Mann emphasizes, is therefore not a minor one. It is a matter of a "fatal imbalance" in the human relation to the planet: the crisis of the Anthropocene.[12]

Capitalism versus the Climate

If natural science has taught us that the rapid pace of anthropogenic climate change threatens to destroy the planet as a home for humanity, then we must turn to social science to understand the social causes of climate change, and the necessary solutions. As a rule, however, the social sciences are compromised from the start. As shown in particular by the discipline of economics, they are ideologically compelled to answer all concrete issues in terms set by capitalism, excluding any perspective that challenges that system or its boundaries. Social scientists are thus discouraged from questioning, or even naming, the fundamental structures and workings of the historical system in which we live.

It follows that the social-scientific contributions most relevant to our understanding of the causes and imperatives of climate change have originated outside the mainstream of academic social science, in critical analyses of capitalism.[13] At issue, as decades of research have demonstrated, is the disjuncture between, on the one hand, the increasing demands put on the environment by a process of ever-expanding capital accumulation, rooted in class, competition, and inequality, and on the other, the capacity of the environment to withstand this assault.[14] The growing pressure on the climate, moreover, is currently taking an especially acute form, due to the system's heavy reliance on fossil-fuel production as a proven engine of capital accumulation worldwide, together with the vested interests of wealth and power that block any transition to renewable forms of energy.

In logical-historical terms, capitalism is a system of capital accumulation, a juggernaut in which each new level of economic growth becomes the mere means to further growth, *ad infinitum*. In the course of its history, capital has been able to "shift" the rifts it has created in the natural metabolism, displacing them elsewhere, often by imposing such externalities on the most vulnerable populations. The capital-accumulation system, however, has now expanded its operations to encompass the entire planet, disrupting the biogeochemical processes of the Earth System itself, most dramatically in the form of climate change. Even though a conversion to renewable energy is hypothetically conceivable within the system, capital's demand for short-term profits, its competitive drive, its vested interests, and its inability to plan for long-term needs all militate against rational energy solutions.[15]

The imperatives of capital accumulation, as analyzed in radical social-science research over the last century and a half (beginning in 1867 with the publication of Karl Marx's *Capital*), are further complicated by the advent, near the end of the last century, of monopoly-finance capital. In this phase the system is characterized by higher levels of global economic concentration, an accumulation regime dominated by financial-asset accumulation and the globalization of production, and a neoliberal political order—giving rise, in some cases, to neo-fascism. Structurally related to this, as an underlying cause, is the stagnation of accumulation in the advanced capitalist economies, and the world economy as a whole.[16] Under this new financialized capitalism, neoliberal policies have sought to remove all regulations on the free flow and amassing of wealth, siphoning more and more of total income into the financial sector, and creating a system of global labor arbitrage or worldwide unequal exchange, the latest phase of imperialism.[17]

All of this is connected in the present historical conjuncture to the declining hegemony of the United States, the rise of China, and attempts to maintain imperial control via the triad of the United States, Europe, and Japan. Elements of the U.S. ruling class, garishly personified by Trump and his advisers, and of the triad as a whole are striving in these circumstances to resurrect national and imperial power through fossil fuels (and nuclear power), military build-ups, financial control, and the repression of immigrants and racially defined "others." They have enlisted in this new but retrograde imperial project parts of a downwardly mobile and demoralized lower-middle class and privileged sectors of the white working class.

This countervailing reaction of a system in peril shows the limits of reform in the epochal crisis—both economic and ecological—in which the world is now entrapped. Reform is only viable under the regime of capital to the extent that it does not come close to threatening the fundamental conditions that govern accumulation as a whole. And well before that point is reached, vested interests normally intervene to stop substantive reforms.[18] The social transformations demanded today by the reality of climate change (as well as economic stagnation) are of such a scale and significance that large sections of these entrenched interests rightly perceive such necessary changes as a danger not only to the immediate prospects for accumulation, and to their own positions of power, but also to the very existence of capitalism, whose importance, in their accounting, outweighs that of the climate itself.[19]

Under these conditions, environmental reforms tend to be too limited to achieve their goals, and even then face unrelenting opposition from fossil-fuel companies and their investors and allies, a category that covers much of the global ruling class. Meanwhile, the almost total failure of centrist-liberal parties and governments, along with their counterparts in the academy, to remove their self-imposed blinders and perceive the reality of capitalism's war on the earth reflects a major moral and ideological default of establishment social science. The result is climate policies that have proven substantially ineffective, and whose implementation represents little more than a loss of precious time amid a rapidly worsening planetary emergency.

It is in the face of this failure of centrist climate policy that Naomi Klein, issuing a wake-up call for the left, famously declared that, at least on this crucial issue, "the right is right." That is, the right is correct in believing that this is a case of "capitalism versus the climate"—though wrong in choosing the former over the latter. So far, in its war on the climate, Klein acknowledges, "capitalism is winning."[20] The system shows no sign of applying the brakes as the runaway train of the profit system hurtles toward the climate precipice. The world's people in these circumstances are mere hostages, unless they should choose to mutiny.

The Failure of Carbon Reform

Over the last few decades, the chief aim of establishment climate-change policy has been the ecological modernization of capitalism, but only within the narrow limits conducive to capital accumulation. This approach is represented at the international level by the Paris Climate Agreement, in which 193 nations came together to sign on to a "plan" to address climate change that, when measured against the present global emergency, is hardly worth the paper on which it is written. The commitments made by individual nations are entirely voluntary and nonbinding, and thus unlikely to be fulfilled, given that there is no overall mechanism for implementation and no worldwide sanctions. And even then, if implemented, these independent national commitments would push the climate well beyond the 2°C barrier, into a world condemned to as much as a 3.7°C increase in global average temperature.[21]

The centerpiece of the Obama administration's climate policy, which formed the basis of the U.S. contribution to the Paris Agreement, was the Clean Power Plan (CPP). Its proponents claimed that it was designed to reduce U.S. carbon emissions by 26–28 percent from 2005 levels by 2025. The CPP consisted chiefly of a set of executive orders extending the Clean Air Act to the regulation of carbon dioxide emissions in electrical power plants, to be implemented by the Environmental Protection Agency (EPA).

Whatever its ambitions, Obama's climate initiative fell far short of the emission reductions that wealthy states would need to introduce if humanity were to maintain a safe and secure relation to the climate. The year 2005 was chosen as the baseline for emission reductions precisely because it represented the peak level of U.S. carbon emissions. As Mark Hertsgaard has pointed out in *The Nation*, the stipulated cuts in U.S. carbon-dioxide emissions, although ostensibly exceeding 25 percent according to the 2005 baseline by 2025, would nonetheless be only 7 percent if measured against the original 1990 baseline of the Kyoto Protocol. The latter agreement mandated that U.S. carbon-dioxide emissions should drop by 7 percent *by 2012*. This original reduction target, which the United States was supposed to have put in place under the Kyoto Protocol but ended up abandoning, was initially conceived in the 1990s as merely a first step in reducing carbon emissions. The CPP's seemingly large projected emissions reductions were thus primarily an outcome of moving the goal posts, with the result that the actual cuts in emissions would still be at a level grossly inadequate to protect humanity from catastrophic climate change, with time fast running out. Further, these prospective reductions would rely primarily on market-friendly carbon-trading schemes that have previously proven ineffective.[22]

The weakness of Obama's centrist-capitalist approach was thrown into stark relief in the *Economic Report of the President* for 2017, where one finds such statements as: "The economic literature suggests that some impacts of climate change, particularly the rise in extreme temperatures, will likely be partly offset by increased private investment in air conditioning, and that movement to avoid temperature extremes, either spending more time indoors in the short run, or relocating in the long run, could also reduce climate impacts on health." Such "Let Them Buy Air Conditioners, Let Them Stay Indoors, and Let Them Move" stances can hardly be considered serious—or ethical—responses to climate change.[23]

Already in 2015, Hansen declared that because the actions outlined in the CPP would "do nothing to attack the fundamental problem," they were "like the fellow who walks to work instead of driving, and thinks he is saving the world." Such measures, he stressed, were "practically worthless." Instead, steps must be taken both nationally and globally to ratchet up the price of carbon and to keep it in the ground. "As long as fossil fuels are allowed to (appear to be) the cheapest energy," and no intervention is made to increase their cost, he continued, "someone will burn them."[24] Ironically, measures designed simply to reduce the demand for carbon in one locale tend only to lower fossil-fuel prices elsewhere (assuming a constant supply of such fuels), thereby ensuring that they will find a market somewhere in the global economy.[25]

It is therefore highly significant that even the meager efforts represented by the Paris Climate Agreement and Obama's Clean Power Plan—which avoided addressing the fundamental problem, and could scarcely be said to pose, at this level, a threat to the system as a whole—nonetheless provoked enormous resistance from the vested interests of fossil-fuel capitalism. Not only did Obama have to circumvent Congress to enact the CPP (and to sign the Paris Agreement, which was possible without congressional approval only because it contained no binding requirements), the whole climate initiative was immediately blocked in court, since the twenty-four states closest to the fossil-fuel industry launched a lawsuit, aided by the U.S. Supreme Court's order that the EPA suspend enforcement of the CPP until a lower court could arrive at a decision. Even this seems a dead letter today, however, since the Trump administration is already seeking to dismantle the CPP and has announced that it will be withdrawing from the Paris Accord.[26]

Trump, in a version of the "big lie," has repeatedly called climate change a "hoax."[27] Accordingly, he has filled the ranks of his transition team and cabinet with climate science denialists and fossil-fuel industry shills. Myron Ebell, director of energy and environmental policy at the Competitive Enterprise Institute and a leading climate contrarian, headed up Trump's transition team. Ebell had publicly accused the respected scientist Kevin Trenberth, a senior climate researcher at the National Center for Atmospheric Research—famous for accounting for the apparent hiatus in global-warming acceleration, using evidence of increased below-surface-level ocean heating—of being "part of a gang" guilty of "cooking the data" on the climate. Financier Anthony Scaramucci, a Trump adviser and an executive member of his transition team, compared the notion of anthropogenic climate change to geocentrism, the belief that the Sun revolves around Earth. In Scaramucci's own words: "I'm saying people have gotten things wrong throughout *the 5,500-year history of our planet*" (italics added). David Schnare, who left the EPA to start an oil industry–funded nonprofit that specialized in suits against the EPA and attacks on climate science, was named to the transition team and charged with revamping the EPA. Schnare gained special notoriety as the attorney who, while working for the right-wing American Tradition Institute (now the Environmental and Energy Legal Institute), targeted both Hansen and Mann, along with other climate scientists, seeking to force them to release private documents and emails. Thomas Pyle, head of the American Energy Alliance, a group with strong links to the oil industry—including Koch Industries, for which he worked as a lobbyist—was chosen to lead the transition team for the Department of Energy. A leaked memo by Pyle lists the immediate goals of the Trump administration's climate policy: (1) withdrawing from the Paris Climate Agreement, (2) dismantling the Clean Power Plan, and (3) expediting approval of pipeline projects.

Trump's choices for major cabinet posts followed the same pattern. Oklahoma Attorney General Scott Pruitt, his pick to lead the EPA, is still another lawyer who has fought the EPA on behalf of the fossil-fuel industry, and is also an outspoken climate-change denier, who wrote in 2016 that the debate on climate change was "far from settled." Ignoring the 97 percent consensus among scientists on the anthropogenic sources of climate change, Pruitt claimed that "scientists continue to disagree about the degree and extent of global warming and its connection to the actions of mankind." Former Texas governor Rick Perry, Trump's pick to head the Department of Energy—a department that, as a Republican presidential contender, Perry promised to eliminate altogether—is a stalwart ally of the fossil-fuel industry. He went so far as to declare in his 2010 book that "we have been experiencing a cooling trend." His administration in Texas deliberately removed all references to climate change in a report addressing rising sea levels. Congressman Ryan Zinke, from coal-producing Montana, Trump's secretary of the interior, likewise asserts that climate change has no firm scientific basis. Attorney General Jeff Sessions has repeatedly insisted, against all evidence, that carbon dioxide is not a pollutant.

Ironically, Trump's secretary of state, Rex Tillerson, previously the CEO of ExxonMobil, stands out in the new administration for his acknowledgment of the reality of climate change. However, as recently as 2013, Tillerson declared that any alternative-energy movement was doomed to fail, and predicted that renewables such as "wind, solar, biofuels," would supply only 1 percent of total energy in 2040. Faced with the demands of environmentalists and protests against the Keystone XL Pipeline, Tillerson simply stated his capitalist creed: "My philosophy is to make money." ExxonMobil under his leadership not only funded climate denialism, but fought to remove all obstacles whatsoever to the increased extraction and burning of fossil fuels.[28]

Most alarming for climate scientists in the first weeks of the Trump transition was a 74-question survey issued in early December to employees in the Energy Department, designed to determine which scientists and officials had been most involved in advancing Obama's Clean Power Plan and other measures to contain climate change. This was widely regarded as the warning shot of a new McCarthyite inquisition against climate scientists, prompting a frantic effort by scientists across the country to archive their data, placing it on widely accessible nongovernmental data bases, lest climate data in government hands be disappeared under Trump. The incoming administration soon disavowed the questionnaire, but the damage was done.[29]

In addition to singling out scientists who advanced Obama's climate initiatives, the questionnaire had a more specific target: the social cost of carbon (SCC), currently estimated at $40 per metric ton, a category used by the Obama administration to quantify the economic impact of climate change and thus to justify the regulation of carbon emissions in cost-benefit terms. The SCC is by now part of established case law and cannot simply be undone. The Trump administration, however, has made clear that it will alter basic premises used to calculate the SCC, such as the discount rate that relates present dollars to future dollars, thereby shrinking the calculation of the costs. Employing a higher discount rate could make the economic costs of climate change appear to vanish, even turn negative, so that climate change appears not only economically benign, but beneficial. In this way the numbers can be manipulated so that any restrictions on greenhouse-gas emissions fail the economic cost-benefit test required by law.[30]

As Hansen usefully pointed out a decade ago, the problem is not the climate denialists as such, since such contrarians, in or out of government, are mere "court jesters" whom no one in the end will take seriously. The problem is "the court" itself, that is,

> the captains of industry, CEOs in fossil fuel companies such as Exxon/Mobil, automobile manufacturers, utilities, all of the leaders who have placed short-term profit above the fate of the planet and the well-being of our children. The court jesters are their jesters, occasionally

> paid for services, and more substantively supported by the captains' disinformation campaigns. . . . The captains of industry are smarter than their jesters. They cannot pretend that they are unaware of climate change dangers and consequences for future generations.[31]

In the new Trump administration fossil-fuel courtiers like Tillerson and their court jesters are now in power, sitting side by side.

It would be wrong, then, to see this administration as simply a cabal of ignoramuses, beginning with the climate-change-denier-in-chief himself. Rather, these efforts to undermine even modest regulations and to discredit sound science are necessary parts of an attempt by carbon capital to proceed undeterred with the burning of fossil fuels, as if this did not constitute a dire threat to the human species. The motive here is quite simply the institutionalized drive for *more*, at virtually any cost to society as a whole. It is analogous, but on a much larger scale, to the decades-long campaign of misinformation by tobacco companies claiming that their products were not killing their customers, even though their own internal scientific research, which they kept hidden, showed the opposite.[32]

Not surprisingly, it is fossil-fuel capital that was the first to benefit from Trump's election. The stocks of oil and gas companies spiked the moment the 2016 election results were announced. Peabody Energy, the leading U.S. coal company, was pulled from the brink of bankruptcy by an immediate 70 percent increase in the value of its shares. Harold Hamm, the billionaire fracking mogul and Trump adviser, indicated that Trump would slash oil and gas drilling regulations: "Every time we can't drill a well in America," Hamm threatens, "terrorism is being funded." For the alt-right website Breitbart News, whose chairman, Steve Bannon, masterminded the later stages of the Trump 2016 presidential campaign (and was later appointed White House chief strategist), there is no global warming, only global cooling. Breitbart greeted Trump's election with the headline: "The Left Just Lost the War on Climate Change."[33]

Significantly, Trump's promise to "build a wall" along the border with Mexico to block "illegal immigration" can be read at least in part as a reaction to climate change, even as the latter is being denied—just as sea walls are hypocritically being proposed by climate deniers in parts of the South as a means to protect coastal real estate. The Trump plan for a more militarized border involves the building of a thousand-mile wall (most of which already exists, in the form of security fences), with the rest of the nearly two-thousand-mile border largely impassable due to natural barriers. The wall would be tightly guarded, monitored by a fleet of aircraft and drones. Here it is impossible not to be reminded of a 2003 Defense Department report, *An Abrupt Climate Change Scenario and Its Implications for United States National Security*, written for the Pentagon by Peter Schwartz and Doug Randall of the Global Business Network, which argued that the catastrophic effects of abrupt climate change would compel wealthy nations like the United States and Australia to construct "defensive fortresses" along their perimeters to shut out climate refugees. "Military confrontation," the report warned, "may be triggered by a desperate need [particularly in the Global South] for natural resources such as energy, food and water," creating new national security threats to which the "have" nations would need to respond—militarily.[34]

The Fire This Time

"Revolution," in the words of Malcolm X, "is like a forest fire. It burns everything in its path. The people who are involved in a revolution don't become a part of the system—they destroy the system, they change the system. The genuine word for a revolution is *Umwälzung*, which means a complete overturning and a complete change. . . . The only way to stop a forest fire from burning down your house is to ignite a fire that you control and use it against the fire that is burning out of control."[35] This controlled backfire is the meaning of counterrevolution. Today virulent anti-environmentalism, tied to a broader neo-fascist politics linked to white supremacy, is the backfire being ignited against both efforts to combat climate change and the larger movement for social and environmental justice.

The urgent task before us in these dire circumstances was explained by Eric S. Godoy and Aaron Jaffe in an op-ed for the *New York Times* in October 2016, headlined "We Don't Need a 'War' on Climate Change, We Need a Revolution." "Following Marx, contemporary [radical ecological] theorists," Godoy and Jaffe note, are investigating "our changing and dangerously unstable metabolic relationship with nature. Humans are a unique species in that we form complex relationships to regulate this metabolism as we produce our food, water, shelter and more robust needs." But the larger reality, of class and social inequality identified with capitalism, means that "the affluent can afford an increase in food prices, ship in bottled water during droughts and relocate businesses and homes when the seas rise, while those without access to such privileges have fewer options and disproportionately suffer." The same logic applies to access to basic technologies and other means of environmental defense. For these and other reasons, climate change endangers the oppressed and underprivileged first, both within nations and globally.

The only conceivable answer today to cascading planetary catastrophe is a broad-based ecological and social revolution, in which the population mobilizes to protect the future of humanity: a revolutionary war for the planet. For Godoy and Jaffe, the "crucial" goal in this respect "is gaining social control over the private, exploitative and even irresponsible direction of the human-nature metabolism," which has generated a metabolic rift in society's relation to the planet. Overcoming this rift requires a majoritarian revolt on a global scale, the likes of which the world has never seen. A "green revolution," they argue, "would center the human-nature metabolism over and against the drive for profits." The goal would be to "transform the relationships that regulate our metabolism with nature, relationships that now allow some to profit by denying this right to others." From this perspective, "Exxon and its climate science obfuscation is not so much an enemy as a paradigmatic symptom of the worst kinds of behavior generated by profit-driven systems. The enemy is the violence perpetrated by [the] racial, gendered, political, juridical and existing economic metabolisms with nature."[36]

Godoy and Jaffe's stance aligns closely with Klein's argument in *This Changes Everything*. Behind the right's climate denial is the economic reality that seriously combatting capitalism's war on the planet requires the defeat of the system. Thus the only alternative for the right and its until-death-do-us-part defenders of capitalism is to invert reality and abandon science. Like Dostoevsky's Underground Man, the right "vomits up reason," rejecting "the laws of nature" and "two times two is four."[37]

The right must deny science and reason precisely because they point to the need for radical social, economic, and ecological transformation. Klein quotes leading British climate scientist Kevin Anderson of the Tyndall Institute for Climate Change Research, who writes that "today, after two decades of bluff and lies, the remaining 2°C budget demands revolutionary change to the political and economic hegemony." As Klein argues, "Revolutionary levels of transformation to the market system" are "now our best hope of avoiding climate chaos."[38]

A world climate movement aimed at countering climate change, Klein states, can be a "galvanizing force for humanity," a "People's Shock, a blow from below," compelling us to create at last the social and economic equality that is so much needed in the world today. She rightly stresses the radical groundswell itself, placing her faith in the leading edge of climate activism, in the form of what she and others call "Blockadia"—a "roving transnational conflict zone" in which climate and environmental-justice activists, indigenous peoples, workers, socialists, and other groups throw up barriers to resist the system.[39]

An example of Blockadia in this sense is the courageous struggle of Native American "water protectors" and their allies, including thousands of military veterans who arrived in the final days to provide a "human shield" at Standing Rock in North Dakota in the summer and fall of 2016. The Standing Rock water protectors endured weeks of state violence in the form of water cannon blasts in freezing temperatures, non-lethal bullets, and tear gas, and succeeded in stopping for a time the construction of the $3.8 billion Dakota Access Pipeline, intended to stretch over a thousand miles from the Bakken and Three Forks production areas in North Dakota, through South Dakota and Iowa, and into Illinois, with the aim of transporting up to 570,000 barrels of oil a day. The pipeline requires drilling under the Missouri River, threatening water supplies due to possible pipeline leakages. The drilling permit was rejected in early December by the Army Corps of Engineers, but was resurrected soon after by the Trump administration, which has made no secret of its determination to see the pipeline completed.[40]

A Two-Stage Ecological Revolution

The primary efforts of radical climate activists in the present historical conjuncture have focused on blocking coal and unconventional fossil fuels, such as oil sands, tight oil, shale gas, oil shale, and oil from ultra-deep-sea wells.[41] This approach is based on a complex climate-change exit strategy articulated most definitively by James Hansen, who has argued that in order to limit the consumption of fossil fuels in today's society while promoting the switch to non-fossil-fuel energy sources, it is necessary to increase the price of fossil fuels substantially through a carbon-fee-and-dividend system. Under such a plan, a fee on carbon, imposed and ratcheted up in stages, would be levied at the mine shaft, wellhead, or point of import, and 100 percent of the funds collected would be redistributed as dividends to families on a per capita basis. The result would be that the vast majority of individuals, with lower carbon footprints at lower income levels, would come out ahead, even under the assumption that the corporations would pass on the full cost of the fees—since the cost net of dividends would fall on those with higher carbon footprints and higher income levels. The beauty of Hansen's scheme is that it could help mobilize humanity as a whole on a class basis with regard to carbon footprints.

However, a higher price for carbon, Hansen insists, is not itself sufficient. It is also necessary to focus on the more dangerous carbon fuels, proscribing their use. Hansen has argued that a key to any exit strategy has to prioritize direct action aimed at shutting down existing coal plants, as well as a moratorium on any new coal plants, and the blocking of the Alberta tar sands—since coal and tar sands oil represent the dirtiest fossil fuels, which could quickly break the global carbon budget. True to his strategy, Hansen has put himself on the line and has been arrested in protests against both coal and tar sands oil.[42]

Nevertheless, the Hansen exit strategy, though influential within the movement, particularly in its call for direct action to block coal and unconventionals, is weakened by its overemphasis on carbon prices. Kevin Anderson has argued that the affluent, who have the highest carbon footprints, can always afford to pay higher carbon prices. More effective would be direct governmental intervention to establish stringent maximum-emissions standards for high-energy-consuming devices. This is not a technological problem, he points out, because the energy-saving and alternative-energy technologies already exist, and in many cases can be immediately substituted at little long-term cost to society as a whole. It does mean, however, confronting the "political and economic hegemony" of the system, including neoclassical economics, which is subservient to the capitalist order.[43]

All of this reflects a narrowing of the options for humanity and the earth. In the current climate conjuncture, the historically necessary ecological and social revolution, in which humanity as a whole would seek once again to take history in its hands, this time to stave off the impending catastrophes of an irrational system, would have to take part in two stages. The first would involve the formation of a broad alliance, modeled after the Popular Front against fascism in the 1930s and '40s. Today's radical alliance would need to be aimed principally at confronting the fossil-fuel–financial complex and its avid right-wing supporters. In this first stage of the struggle, manifold demands could be made and broadly agreed on within the existing system—ways of eliminating carbon emissions and economic waste while also promoting social and environmental needs—which, although inimical to the logic of capital, and particularly to the fossil-fuel industry, would not necessarily call into immediate question the existence of the capitalist system itself.[44]

However, in the long run, capitalism's threat to planetary boundaries cannot be solved by stopgap reforms, however radical, that leave the system's fundamental features intact while simply transcending its relation to fossil fuels. The danger to the planetary environment posed by the accumulation of capital is all-encompassing.[45] This means that the ecological revolution will have to extend eventually to the roots of production itself, and will have to assume the form of a system of substantive equality for all: racial freedom, gender and LGBTQ equality, a classless society, an end to imperialism, and the protection of the earth for future generations.

In the long run, the struggle is therefore synonymous with the movement toward socialism. The more revolutionary the struggle, the more it is likely to emanate from those whose needs are greatest, and thus from the Global South. It is in the periphery of the system, rather than in the center, that humanity is most likely to mutiny against the existing order. Hope today therefore lies first and foremost in the revolt of "the wretched of the earth," opening up fissures at the center of the system itself.

But even if all of this were to fail and our present hopes were to go unrealized, with the world pushed to the planetary turning point, it would remain true, then as now, that the only answer is ecological and social revolution. There is no next time. *It is the fire this time.*[46]

The Nature of the Resistance: A Brief Conclusion

> All progress in the writing of modern history has been effected by descending from the political surface into the depths of social life.
>
> —KARL MARX[1]

DURING A WHITE HOUSE CELEBRATION of Israel Independence Day on May 2, 2017, Steve Bannon was photographed standing in front of a now famous whiteboard on which all of Donald Trump's campaign promises were written out in longhand. Next to Bannon in the photo was the American Rabbi Shmuley Boteach, a frequent contributor to Breitbart, known for his virulent support for Israel and opposition to the Palestinians and for his advocacy of a U.S. war on Syria and Iran. In what was clearly an orchestrated move in conjunction with Bannon, Boteach immediately tweeted the photo, where it quickly went viral and was picked up by the major media.[2]

In the carefully staged photo, Bannon was shown standing on one side of the whiteboard in front of the "Pledges on Obamacare," and Trump's "Pledges on Immigration" could clearly be seen to Bannon's left. Checked off were such items as "Suspend immigration from terror-prone regimes";

"Implement new extreme immigration vetting techniques"; "Suspend the Syrian Refugee Program"; "Issue detainees for all illegal immigrants who are arrested for any crime and they will be placed into immediate removal proceedings"; "Hire 5,000 more border patrol agents"; and "Triple the number of ICE [Immigration and Custom Enforcement] agents." Listed but not yet checked off was "Build the border wall and eventually make Mexico pay for it." The aim of all of this was to signal to Trump's white lower-middle class and relatively privileged white working-class supporters that he was determined to keep his campaign promises, and that he was on their side against immigrants, refugees, and other marginalized groups.

But a key Breitbart article on Bannon's whiteboard also made it clear that Trump administration goals included promises to monopoly-finance capital. Listed on the whiteboard under "Pledges on Tax Reform," according to Breitbart, but not visible in the photo itself, were "Lower the corporate tax to 15 percent" and "Eliminate the estate tax."[3] These pledges, together with the others on immigration, testified to the dangerous and unpredictable alliance forged between a reactionary lower-middle class and monopoly-finance capital, constituting neo-fascism as a new political order in the making.

The argument in this book is that complacency in the face of the nascent neo-fascist shift in U.S. politics would be a grave error. Perhaps the most profound critique of this radical right threat in U.S. politics has emanated from the eminent political scientist Walter Dean Burnham, author of *The Current Crisis in American Politics* and the foremost analyst of critical alignments in U.S. politics.[4] More than four decades ago, in 1972, in the aftermath of George Wallace's independent white supremacist presidential campaign, Burnham argued that the U.S. political order exhibited many of the weaknesses, in terms of vulnerability to the rise of fascist political movements, that had characterized Germany's Weimar Republic prior to Hitler's rise to power.[5] The crucial factor here was the predominantly white lower-middle-class/upper-working-class strata, corresponding to "the bulk of the *petite bourgeoisie* in the traditional European class structure." Here Burnham quoted Marx and Engels from *The Communist Manifesto*: "The lower-middle class, the small manufacturer, the shopkeeper, the artisan, the peasant—all these fight against the bourgeoisie, to save from extinction their existence as fractions of the middle class. They are therefore not revolutionary, but conservative. Nay, more, they are reactionary, for they try to roll back the wheel of history."[6]

Commenting on this declaration by Marx and Engels, Burnham wrote:

> In more neutral language, it can be said of such strata that they are less actors than acted upon by social transformations which threaten without enlightening them; that they are dependent, vulnerable, and politically reactive under stress; and that, lacking a preexisting political church which explains their plight to them, their instinctive response to dangerously stressful social change is to support those candidates and movements who can most effectively promise them that such change will be stopped. As the traditional bourgeois-liberal *Honoriatorenpartei* [a party controlled by political elites, lacking a clearly defined program or basis of mass participation outside the vote] is the characteristic vehicle of lower-middle class expression in stable times, so the fascist movement corresponds to the political church which emerges to embrace these strata as a refuge from damaging change in their social environment.[7]

Returning to his argument in 2016 in response to the Trump campaign, Burnham observed in "Breitbart, Steven Bannon and Donald Trump Against the World" that Trumpism is not an aberration, but rather reflects the deeper reality that there has long been "an embedded instability in American politics," pointing to the "potential for large-scale 'jumping overboard' toward right-wing extremist political movements." This reflected a "general legitimacy crisis of the entire American regime order."[8] What finally brought these submerged political tendencies to the fore was "the financial meltdown of 2008, leading to interventions by state actors to prevent an outright depression, [and] the elevation of the first African-American president." Trump, according to Burnham, "began his political career . . . by a years'-long insistence that President Barack Obama was literally an 'alien other.'" As early as June 2015, Trump's political thrust was "squarely focused on the less-educated, lower-middle/white working class, major victims of policies pursued by the established elites of both parties." Linked to this was Trump's political "elevation of Steve Bannon, creator of Breitbart Media, and a leading figure of the 'alt-right.'"[9]

As we have seen in the foregoing chapters, there is little doubt that Bannon and Breitbart represent the emergence of a full-fledged neo-fascist politics. Indeed, the rise of the radical right as the most combative sector of Trumpism helps us to situate Trump himself, based on the old adage that one can judge people by the company they keep. Bannon, as Trump's campaign manager and chief White House strategist, masterminded a neo-fascist, that is, racist, ultra-nationalist, patriarchal, and financial-capitalist, path to power, well in keeping with Trump's own views. Moreover, Bannon and other Breitbart figures in the Trump White House demonstrate considerable knowledge of and affinity for today's transnational neo-fascist movements emerging in Europe.

Trumpism is thus not to be regarded as an accidental or ephemeral movement—regardless of the eventual political fate of Trump himself, who is presently beleaguered by Russiagate investigations throwing the future of his administration into question. The neo-fascist monster once released on the world will not easily go away. Rather it is a definite manifestation of the crisis of the U.S. imperial economy, emanating both from the deepening of the economic stagnation of monopoly-finance capital and the gradual erosion of U.S. economic hegemony.

A characteristic of Trump himself, congruent with the movement he represents, is a chauvinistic view of people of color, immigrants, and women, evident in his long string of racist and misogynist statements. He is a dedicated enemy of the wider working class, including the poor and marginalized populations.[10] He has encouraged white supremacism, neo-fascism, and hatred toward all "Others." From the start, this was largely tolerated by the mainstream media, the political establishment, and the capitalist class. Trump's racism and misogyny were generally passed off as the personal foibles of a tawdry billionaire celebrity, not as representing a dangerous political tendency, even when it became apparent that these dark outpourings were formative aspects of the political movement rapidly developing around him. This mainstream legitimization of Trumpism most often took the form of presenting it as a relatively harmless "right-wing populism," rather than as constituting a neo-fascist political movement that would inevitably challenge the separation of powers within the state, civil liberties, and the forms of democratic rule.

The reasons for this handling of Trump with kid gloves are clear. Movements in the fascist genus have always represented the rearguard defense of capitalism, the most virulent enemy of the socialist left. They are thus seen as natural allies of the center right, particularly in times of growing political and economic instability. Trumpism has fed on an anti-leftist great fear, which has grown in intensity as a result of the white supremacist response to Barack Obama's neoliberal presidency, as well as concerns at the top regarding an emerging economic populism.[11] Trumpism's rise has thus gone hand-in-hand with an enormous upsurge throughout the country of hate crimes, including outpourings of hatred against people of color, women, LGBTQ people, immigrants, and the poor.[12] This reflects the anger and distress of the lower-middle class. But behind the even greater worries among the moneyed interests is the specter of a class-based socialist alternative that could meld together the various movements from below symbolized by the "99 percent movement" launched by Occupy.[13]

It was clearly such trepidations over a united left groundswell eventually emerging in response to conditions of economic stagnation, financialization (including widespread indebtedness), soaring inequality, declining U.S. hegemony, permanent war, ecological catastrophe, and the neoliberal micromanaging of the expropriation of the population that led the powers that be to throw their support at least partly to Trumpism, seeing it as necessary element in the defense of their economic interests. Like other similar neo-fascist developments in Europe, Trumpism is viewed by the capitalist Masters of the Universe and their hangers-on as a phenomenon that could help stabilize plutocratic rule.

If there is an actual basis for these right-wing, capitalist fears of the left in the United States today, it is to be found not in the weak precedent set by the neoliberal Obama administration, with its meager and contradictory efforts to promote "equal opportunity" while at the same time encouraging skyrocketing inequality. Rather, it lies in the realization among the well-to-do that the crisis of the U.S. state and society had reached the point that a genuine, uncompromising movement toward socialism might well emerge. A clear manifestation of this potential threat to the dominant social relations was Bernie Sanders's extraordinarily powerful 2016 presidential campaign as an acknowledged "socialist" or social democrat. Sanders's progress through the Democratic primaries was a political earthquake, the tremors of which were felt across the country, and especially at the pinnacles of power. Unlike Clinton and Trump, Sanders received no support from the capitalist class, and had no wealth on which to rely. Nevertheless, Sanders proved to be close to unstoppable as millions flocked to his political standard.

The Sanders campaign thus pointed to a potential class-political struggle unlike any seen since the 1930s. Poll after poll showed he would have decisively beaten Trump.[14] Sanders was particularly strong in the Rust Belt states that sealed Clinton's Electoral College defeat to Trump. As one insightful commentator noted, a workerist social democrat like "Sanders would be Kryptonite for a pseudo-populist like Trump."[15] Yet Sanders was blocked by a Democratic Party establishment and an undemocratic system of super delegates.[16] Further, in a political contradiction that may have proven fatal, he was unable to draw sufficient African American voters away from their decades-long alliance with the Clinton political machine.[17]

To be sure, a Sanders victory would not in itself have transformed the political-economic power relations in Washington. He would have had no support within the Democratic Party establishment, the state as a whole, or the ruling class, and would have lacked any institutionalized bases of political power anywhere in the society, since there is at present no organized movement at the ground level on which he could have relied. Nevertheless, what the Sanders campaign exposed was the unconscious (and sometimes even conscious) socialist groundswell at the base of U.S. society, and an urgent, desperate need for a new beginning. It became clear that the only answer to neoliberalism and neo-fascism in the present age is a reemergent socialism able to address the endless crisis of capitalism itself.

A genuine socialist political movement of any significance in the twenty-first century—given capitalism's epochal economic and environmental crises, its deepening, multifaceted forms of oppression, and its proclivity toward ever-expanding wars—would have to be a revolutionary one, rooted in construction of alternative bases of power, organized resistance, and grassroots revolt. This means massive, organized, *extra-electoral* mobilization among the great majority of the society, particularly labor, bound together within a broad "co-revolutionary" coalition.[18]

The ultimate condition for a genuine socialist resistance movement in the United States today, given the U.S. position as the hegemonic power in the imperialist world system, together with its gradual erosion, is *anti-imperialism* rooted in international solidarity. It is the revolt against imperialism that constitutes the Achilles' heel of the entire system. As the platform of the Movement for Black Lives declares, "We know that patriarchy, exploitative capitalism, militarism, and white supremacy know no borders. We stand in solidarity with our international family against the ravages of global capitalism and anti-Black racism, human-made climate change, war, and exploitation."[19] Inseparable from this is the commencement of the real struggle for the defense of the planetary environment. If the System Change Not Climate Change movement were to gain real momentum in the United States, at the center of the imperialist world system, it could serve to remove some of the chains currently imposed on earth struggles already being fought against enormous odds around the globe, often led by indigenous peoples.

It is the movement for a New International of the associated producers and of the peoples of the earth that constitutes the greatest threat to today's imperial governance and the financial capitalist plutocracy that it supports, and the greatest challenge facing human liberation. What is needed, then, is a truly global socialism, based on ecological sustainability and substantive equality: a world of freedom in general.

Notes

Preface

1. Sofia Tesfaye, "Trump's Bloody Boast: I Could Shoot Somebody and I Wouldn't Lose Voters," Salon.com, January 25, 2016.
2. Naomi Klein, *No Is Not Enough: Resisting Trump's Shock Politics* (Chicago: Haymarket Books, 2017), 33–34.
3. See Georg Lukács, *The Destruction of Reason* (London: Merlin Press, 1980), the classic work on the philosophical origins of fascist ideology. On "ecocidal capitalism" see Klein, *No Is Not Enough*, 228.

1. Neo-Fascism in the White House

1. Epigraph: Jack London, *The Iron Heel* (Chicago: Lawrence Hill Books, 1907), 67–68.
2. For earlier treatments of neo-fascism in the United States since the election see "Cornel West on Donald Trump: This Is What Neo-Fascism Looks Like," *Democracy Now!,* December 1, 2016; Henry A. Giroux, "Combating Trump's Neo-Fascism and the Ghost of '1984,'" Truthout, February 7, 2017. U.S. neo-fascism can be seen, in the words of Paul A. Baran, as "a fascism sui generis, of a special American variety." Baran, writing as Historicus, "Rejoinder," *Monthly Review* 4/12 (April 1953): 503. The notion of "neo-fascism" first arose in accounts of extreme New Right movements and ideologies in Europe associated with thinkers such as Julius Evola and Alain de Benoist. See Roger Griffin, ed., *Fascism* (Oxford: Oxford University Press, 1995), 311–16.
3. CNN, "Exit Polls, Election 2016," November 23, 2016, http://cnn.com.
4. Jonathan Rothwell and Pablo Diego-Rosell, "Explaining Nationalist Political Views: The Case of Donald Trump," Gallup draft

working paper, November 2, 2016, available at http://papers.ssrn.com, 12; Samantha Neal, "Why Trump's Base Differs from the Typical Republican Crowd," Huffington Post, August 22, 2016, http://www.huffingtonpost.com/entry/trump-base-different-from-republicans_us_57ae4c2ee4b069e7e5057715.

5. Konstantin Kilibarda and Daria Roithmayr, "The Myth of the Rust Belt Revolt," Slate, December 1, 2016.
6. CNN, "Exit Polls, Election 2016."
7. Jason Horowitz, "Donald Trump Jr.'s Skittles Tweet Fits a Pattern," *New York Times*, September 20, 2016.
8. Rothwell and Diego-Rosell, "Explaining Nationalist Political Views," 2.
9. Richard F. Hamilton, *Who Voted for Hitler?* (Princeton: Princeton University Press, 1982), 420. Hamilton says it is impossible to confirm (or deny) the decisive role of lower-middle-class voters based on the available data on electoral outcomes for urban areas in Germany in 1931 and 1932, though his own data could be interpreted as supporting this. Nevertheless, the fact that fascism was historically rooted in the lower-middle class or petty bourgeoisie is one of the most firmly established observations in the entire literature on fascism's rise, both in the 1930s and today, encompassing both Marxist and non-Marxist thinkers. See, for example, Nicos Poulantzas, *Fascism and Dictatorship* (London: Verso, 1974); Seymour Martin Lipset, *Political Man* (New York: Doubleday, 1960), 134–76. Leon Trotsky wrote that "fascism is a specific means of mobilising and organising the petty bourgeoisie in the social interests of finance capital." Leon Trotsky, *The Struggle Against Fascism in Germany* (New York: Pathfinder, 1971), 455.
10. Michael H. Kater, *The Nazi Party* (Cambridge, MA: Harvard University Press, 1983), 252; Thomas Childers, *The Nazi Voter* (Chapel Hill: University of North Carolina Press, 1983), 157–59, 166–88, 225–26; Jürgen W. Falter, "How Likely Were Workers to Vote for the NSDAP?," in *The Rise of National Socialism and the Working Classes in Weimar Germany*, ed. Conan Fischer (Providence, RI: Berghan Books, 1996), 9–45.
11. Trump was never very isolated from the financial community and billionaire class, of course. See Robert Hackett, "Here Are the Billionaires Supporting Trump," *Fortune*, August 3, 2016.
12. Paul Baran argued in the 1950s that the absence of these fac-

tors did not necessarily prevent the growth of fascism in a U.S. context. One should not confuse the objective tendencies with its outward forms, or expect a social phenomenon to manifest itself always in the same way. Baran, "Fascism in America," 181. Similarly, Bertram Gross wrote, "Anyone looking for black shirts, mass parties, or men on horseback will miss the telltale clues of creeping fascism." Bertram Gross, *Friendly Fascism* (New York: Evans, 1980), 3.

13. Donald Trump, "Inaugural Address," January 20, 2017, http://whitehouse.gov. On "palingenetic ultra-nationalism" as the matrix of fascist ideology see Roger Griffin, "General Introduction," in Griffin, *Fascism*, 3–4. On "The Potentially Deadliest Phase of Imperialism," see István Mészáros, *The Necessity of Social Control* (New York: Monthly Review Press, 2015), 97–120.
14. *Bulletin of Atomic Scientists,* "It Is Two and a Half Minutes to Midnight," news release, January 25, 2017, http://thebulletin.org/press-release/it-now-two-and-half-minutes-midnight10432.
15. Louis Althusser, *Lenin and Philosophy and Other Essays* (New York: Monthly Review Press, 2001), 85–126.
16. Richard Falk, "The Dismal Cartography of Trump's Pre-Fascist State (and Opportunities for Progressive Populism)," Mondoweiss, January 26, 2017, http://mondoweiss.net/2017/01/cartography-opportunities-progressive/.
17. Samir Amin, "The Return of Fascism in Contemporary Capitalism," *Monthly Review* 66/4 (September 2014): 1–12.
18. See C. B. Macpherson, *The Life and Times of Liberal Democracy* (Oxford: Oxford University Press, 1977); Paul A. Baran and Paul M. Sweezy, *Monopoly Capital* (New York: Monthly Review Press, 1966), 155; Ralph Miliband, *The State in Capitalist Society* (London: Quartet, 1969).
19. Michael D. Yates, *The Great Inequality* (London: Routledge, 2016).
20. Bertolt Brecht, *Brecht on Theatre* (London: Methuen, 1974), 47.
21. Paul M. Sweezy to Paul M. Baran, October 18, 1952, in Baran and Sweezy, *The Age of Monopoly Capital* (New York: Monthly Review Press, 2017), 86–87.
22. Paul A. Baran to Paul M. Sweezy, October 25, 1952, in ibid, 92–93. Although fascism tends to reduce the state to one principle, it is conceivable, Baran noted in this letter, that it could take the form of "parliamentary fascism," that is, it need not inherently be organized around the executive power. "The crucial point," he

wrote, "is that terrorism, oppressiveness, *Gleichschaltung* [synchronization], state domination, etc. etc. are introduced in a specific class struggle constellation."

23. As Chris Hedges notes, "Hitler, days after he took power in 1933, imposed a ban on all homosexual and lesbian organizations. He ordered raids on places where homosexuals gathered, culminating in the ransacking of the Institute for Sexual Science in Berlin, and the permanent exile of its director, Magnus Hirschfeld. Thousands of volumes from the institute's library were tossed into a bonfire. The stripping of gay and lesbian Germans of their civil rights was largely cheered by the German churches. But this campaign legitimated tactics, outside the law, that would soon be employed by others." Chris Hedges, *American Fascists* (New York: Free Press, 2006), 201. See also Ralf Dose, *Magnus Hirschfeld* (New York: Monthly Review Press, 2014).

24. See Franz Neumann, *Behemoth* (New York: Oxford University Press, 1942), 62–82. This is the classic account of the development of the Nazi state and its relation to the economy. Although the "totalitarian state"—not to be confused with the later liberal concept of "totalitarianism"—is the ideal of fascism, in actuality it was less monolithic, and more chaotic. In classical fascism, a "dual state" consisting of the state apparatus and the party apparatus was typical, and the centralization of state power did not prevent a kind of disarticulation, in which the state ceased to function fully as a state in all respects, no longer accomplishing all of the tasks of Thomas Hobbes's *Leviathan*. For this reason, Neumann took the title of his work on fascism from Hobbes's *Behemoth*, which was on the period of the Long Parliament. See Neumann, *Behemoth*, 459–60; Slavoj Žižek, *Did Somebody Say Totalitarianism?* (London: Verso, 2001), 1–3.

25. Poulantzas refers to the fascist state as "relatively autonomous" from monopoly capital. It seems more appropriate to reverse the emphasis and to refer to the economy and monopoly capital as strongly autonomous. Monopoly capital prefers a liberal democratic state but is willing to accede to fascist management of the political economy as long as private, monopolistic capital accumulation is allowed to continue and is even enhanced within the fascist "superstructural" framework. See Poulantzas, *Fascism and Dictatorship*, 85. In Nazi Germany this strong autonomy of capital was only interfered with in the midst of the war, when Albert

Speer was put in charge of organizing industry for the war effort. See Franz Neumann and Paul M. Sweezy, "Speer's Appointment as Dictator of the German Economy," in Franz Neumann, Herbert Marcuse, and Otto Kirchheimer, *Secret Reports on Nazi Germany* (Princeton: Princeton University Press, 2013), 48–60.

26. Benito Mussolini, "Plan for the New Italian Economy (1936)," in *Economic Fascism,* ed. Carlo Celli (Edinburgh, VA: Axios, 2013), 277–80.
27. Hitler quoted in Konrad Heiden, *Der Fuehrer* (Boston: Houghton Mifflin, 1944), 287; Robert W. McChesney and John Nichols, *People Get Ready* (New York: Nation Books, 2016), 38.
28. Maxine Y. Sweezy (also under Maxine Y. Woolston), *The Structure of the Nazi Economy* (Cambridge, MA: Harvard University Press, 1941), 27–35. See also Gustav Stolper, *German Economy, 1870–1940* (New York: Reynal and Hitchcock, 1940), 207; Germà Bel, "The Coining of 'Privatization' and Germany's National Socialist Party," *Journal of Economic Perspectives* 20/3 (2006): 187–94, and "Against the Mainstream: Nazi Privatization in 1930s Germany," University of Barcelona, Research Study, no date, http://www.ub.edu/graap/nazi.pdf.
29. Nicos Poulantzas, *Fascism and Dictatorship* (London: Verso, 1974), 344.
30. Karl Dietrich Bracher, "Stages of Totalitarian 'Integration' (*Gleichschaltung*): The Consolidation of National Socialist Rule in 1933 and 1934," in *Republic to Reich,* ed. Hajo Holborn (New York: Vintage, 1972), 109–28; Robert O. Paxton, *The Anatomy of Fascism* (New York: Vintage, 2005), 123–24; Emmanuel Faye, *Heidegger* (New Haven: Yale University Press, 2009), 39–58.
31. Faye, *Heidegger*, 151–54; Carl Schmitt, "The Legal Basis of the Total State," in Griffin, *Fascism*, 138–39.
32. Bracher, "Stages of Totalitarian 'Integration,'" 118–22. On the Reichstag fire, see John Mage and Michael E. Tigar, "The Reichstag Fire Trial, 1933–2008," *Monthly Review* 60/10 (March 2009): 24–49.
33. Bracher, "Stages of Totalitarian 'Integration,'" 122–24.
34. Faye, *Heidegger*, 39–53, 118,154–62, 316–22; Richard Wolin, ed., *The Heidegger Controversy* (Cambridge, MA: MIT Press, 1993).
35. Bracher, "Stages of Totalitarian 'Integration,'" 124–28. Here, what Bracher called the third and fourth stages of *Gleichschaltung* in the German case are treated as one.

36. Paxton, *Anatomy of Fascism*, 123.
37. See Oliver Staley, "There's a German Word that Perfectly Encapsulates the Start of Trump's Presidency," Quartz, January 26, 2017, https://qz.com/895436/gleichschaltung-the-german-word-that-perfectly-encapsulates-the-start-of-trumps-presidency/; Shawn Hamilton, "What Those Who Studied Nazis Can Teach Us about the Strange Reaction to Donald Trump," Huffington Post, December 19, 2016, http://www.huffingtonpost.com/entry/donald-trump-nazi-propaganda-coordinate_us_58583b6fe4b08debb78a7d5c; Ron Jacobs, "Trumpism's Gleichschaltung?," Counterpunch, February 3, 2017, https://www.counterpunch.org/2017/02/03/trumpisms-gleichschaltung/.
38. Amin, "The Return of Fascism," 2.
39. Trump, "Inaugural Address"; Joseph Stiglitz, "How to Survive the Trump Era," Project Syndicate, February 20, 2017, http://project-syndicate.org; "Miller and Bannon Wrote Trump Inaugural Address," The Hill, January 21, 2017, http://thehill.com/homenews/administration/315464-bannon-miller-wrote-trumps-inauguration-address-report.
40. According to *Vanity Fair*, in August 2016, "Bannon . . . expressed a wariness about the political genuineness of Trump's campaign persona. Trump is a 'blunt instrument for us. . . . I don't know whether he really gets it or not.'" Ken Stern, "Exclusive: Stephen Bannon, Trump's New C.E.O., Hints at His Master Plan," *Vanity Fair*, August 17, 2016.
41. Andrew Marantz, "Becoming Steve Bannon's Bannon," *The New Yorker*, February 13, 2017.
42. Gwynn Guilford and Nikhil Sonnad, "What Steve Bannon Really Wants," Quartz, February 3, 2017, https://qz.com/898134/what-steve-bannon-really-wants/; Steve Reilly and Brad Heath, "Steve Bannon's Own Words Show Sharp Break on Security," *USA Today*, January 31, 2017.
43. Steve Bannon, remarks via Skype at the Human Dignity Conference, the Vatican, Summer 2014, transcribed in J. Lester Feeder, "This Is How Steve Bannon Sees the World," Buzzfeed, November 15, 2016, https://www.buzzfeed.com/lesterfeder/this-is-how-steve-bannon-sees-the-entire-world?utm_term=.onWBXJXod#.sl5Bmrm0X.
44. Bannon, ibid.; Jason Horowitz, "Steve Bannon Cited Italian Thinker Who Inspired Fascists," *New York Times*, February 10, 2017.

45. Julius Evola, "Fascism: Myth and Reality" and "The True Europe's Revolt Against the Modern World," in Griffin, *Fascism*, 317–18, 342–44; Paul Furlong, *Social and Political Thought of Julius Evola* (London: Routledge, 2011), 77, 89. Umberto Eco has called Evola "one of the most respected fascist gurus." Umberto Eco, "Ur-Fascism," *New York Review of Books*, June 22, 1995.
46. Bannon, remarks at the Human Dignity Conference.
47. Anjali Singhvi and Alicia Parlapiano, "Trump's Immigration Ban: Who Is Barred and Who Is Not," *New York Times*, February 3, 2017; Ben Rosen, "Up Close and Personal: How Trump's Attacks Against the Judiciary Are Different," *Christian Science Monitor*, February 9, 2017.
48. Philip Rucker and Robert Barnes, "Trump to Inherit More than 100 Court Vacancies, Plans to Reshape Judiciary," *Washington Post*, December 25, 2016; ABC News, "Trump's Order May Mark 11 Million Undocumented Immigrants for Deportation: Experts," January 26, 2017, http://abcnews.go.com/Politics/trumps-order-mark-11-million-undocumented-immigrants-deportation/story?id=45050901; Donald Trump, "Remarks by President Trump in Joint Address to Congress," February 28, 2017.
49. Donald Trump, "Presidential Memorandum: Organization of the National Security Council and the Homeland Security Council," January 28, 2017; Edward Price, "I Didn't Think I Would Ever Leave the CIA," *Washington Post*, February 20, 2017, https://www.washingtonpost.com/opinions/i-didnt-think-id-ever-leave-the-cia-but-because-of-trump-i-quit/2017/02/20/fd7aac3e-f456-11e6-b9c9-e83fce42fb61_story.html?utm_term=.5f7e7251dd6c; Linda Qiu, "The National Security Council 'Shakeup,'" Politifact, February 1, 2017.
50. Josh Dawsey, "Trump's Advisers Push Him to Purge Obama Appointees," Politico, March 3, 2017, http://www.politico.com/story/2017/03/trump-obama-appointees-advisers-purge-235629.
51. Philip Rucker and Robert Costa, "Bannon Vows a Daily Fight for 'Deconstruction of the Administrative State,'" *Washington Post*, February 23, 2017; BBC, "Trump Adviser Hails 'New Political Order,'" February 23, 2017, http://www.bbc.com/news/world-us-canada-39059990.
52. Chris Arnold, "President Trump to Cut Regulations by 75 Percent,'" National Public Radio, January 24, 2017, http://www.

npr.org/2017/01/24/511341779/president-trump-to-cut-regulations-by-75-percent-how-real-is-that.

53. Damian Carrington, "Green Movement 'Greatest Threat to Freedom,' Says Trump Adviser," *Guardian*, January 30, 2017.

54. Henry Fountain, "Trump's Climate Contrarian: Myron Ebell Takes on the E.P.A.," *New York Times*, November 11, 2016.

55. Carrington, "Green Movement 'Greatest Threat to Freedom'"; Penny Lewis, "What's Coming for Unions Under President Trump," *Labor Notes*, January 19, 2017; Matthew Rozsa, "House Republicans Support Rule that Could Allow Them to Pay Individual Federal Workers $1," Salon, January 6, 2017, http://www.salon.com/2017/01/06/house-republicans-support-rule-that-could-allow-them-to-pay-individual-federal-workers-1/; Rafi Letzter, "Trump's Budget Could Cut 3,000 Staff from the EPA, Report Suggests," Business Insider, March 1, 2017, http://www.businessinsider.com/trump-budget-epa-layoff-2017-3; "White House Proposes Steep Budget Cut to Leading Climate Science Agency," *Washington Post*, March 3, 2017.

56. David Pluviose, "Cornel West: We're All Responsible for Gangster Trump," Diverse, January 25, 2017, http://divereducation.com.

57. Eric Tucker, "Sessions: US to Continue Use of Privately Run Prisons," Associated Press, February 23, 2017; CNN, "Donald Trump Defends Racial Profiling in Wake of Bombings," September 19, 2016; CBS News, "Donald Trump: Black Lives Matter Calls for Killing Police," July 19, 2016; John Hayward, "Petition to Designate Black Lives Matter as Terrorist Group Approaches 100K Signatures," Breitbart, July 11, 2016, http://breitbart.com.

58. Lewis, "What's Coming for Unions"; Michael Paarlberg, "With All Eyes on Trump Republicans Are Planning to Break Unions for Good," *Guardian*, February 2, 2017.

59. Politico, "Labor Nominee Acosta: Trump Is the Boss," March 22, 2017, http://www.politico.com/story/2017/03/alexander-acosta-donald-trump-labor-hearing-236377.

60. Kevin Carey, "Why Betsy DeVos Won't Be Able to Privatize U.S. Education," *New York Times*, November 23, 2016; Kristina Rizga, "Betsy DeVos Wants to Use America's Schools to Build 'God's Kingdom,'" *Mother Jones*, March/April 2017.

61. Amy X. Wang, "Trump Is Picking Free-Speech Fight with the University that Birthed the Free Speech Movement," Quartz, February 2, 2017, https://qz.com/901215/can-a-president-

pull-funding-from-a-university-trump-picks-a-free-speech-fight-with-berkeley-the-college-that-birthed-the-free-speech-movement/; Abby Ohlheiser, "Just How Offensive Did Milo Yiannopoulos Have to Be to Get Banned from Twitter?," *Washington Post*, July 21, 2016. Yiannopoulos resigned from Breitbart in mid-February 2017 amid a growing scandal over his active promotion of pederasty.

62. Max Greenwood, "Trump Tweets: The Media Is the 'Enemy of the American People,'" The Hill, February 17, 2017, http://thehill.com/homenews/administration/320168-trump-the-media-is-the-enemy-of-the-american-people.
63. David Bauder, "Trump's 'Running War' on the Media Undermines Trust," Associated Press, January 23, 2017. Edward Herman, "The Propaganda Model Revisited," in *Capitalism and the Information Age*, ed. Robert W. McChesney, Ellen Meiksins Wood, and John Bellamy Foster (New York: Monthly Review Press, 1998), 191–205.
64. Michael M. Grynbaum, "Trump Strategist Stephen Bannon Says Media 'Should Keep Its Mouth Shut,'" *New York Times*, January 26, 2017; Jim Rutenberg, "In Trump Era, Censorship May Start in the Newsroom," *New York Times*, February 17, 2017.
65. Danielle Kurtzleben, "The Trump Media Survey Is Phenomenally Biased. It's Also Useful," National Public Radio, February 17, 2017.
66. Lukas I. Alpert, "Some Media Excluded from White House Briefing," *Wall Street Journal*, February 24, 2017.
67. Grant Stern, "My Mouth Is Shut, So You Can Read Steve Bannon's Words; He Runs America Now," Huffington Post, January 30, 2017, http://www.huffingtonpost.com/entry/my-mouth-is-shut-so-you-can-read-steve-bannons-words_us_588e0fe5e4b0cd25e49049f8.
68. Rucker and Costa, "Bannon Vows a Daily Fight"; Max Fisher, "Stephen K. Bannon's CPAC Comments, Annotated and Explained," *New York Times*, February 24, 2017.
69. Daniel Horowitz, "Trump's Executive Orders for American Sovereignty Are Game Changers," *Conservative Review*, January 25, 2017, http://conservativereview.com; "7 Steps to Reclaiming Our Sovereignty," Breitbart, July 17, 2014, http://www.breitbart.com/big-government/2014/07/17/7-steps-to-reclaiming-our-sovereignty/; Nick Hallet, "Eurosceptic Parties Sign 'Stockholm Declaration' Pledging to Defend Sovereignty, Defeat Radical

Islam," Breitbart, November 5, 2016, http://www.breitbart.com/london/2016/11/05/eurosceptic-parties-sign-declaration-pledging-defend-sovereignty-defeat-radical-islam/. See also Furlong, *Social and Political Thought of Julius Evola*, 77.

70. Robert Costa, "Trump's Latest Hire Alarms Allies of Ryan—and Bolsters Bannon," *Washington Post*, January 33, 2017; Marantz, "Becoming Steve Bannon's Bannon"; Bill Moyers and Michael Winship, "Donald Trump's Mission Creep Just Took a Giant Leap Forward," *Moyers and Company*, February 1, 2017, http://billmoyers.com/story/donald-trumps-mission-creep-just-took-giant-leap-forward/.
71. Barack Obama, "Statement by the President on H.R. 1540," December 31, 2011, http://obamawhitehouse.archives.gov; Jean-Claude Paye, "Sovereignty and the State of Emergency," *Monthly Review* 68/8 (January 2017): 1–11; Carl Mirra, "The NDAA and the Militarization of America," Foreign Policy in Focus, February 10, 2012, http://fpif.org; Michael E. Tigar, "The National Security State: The End of Separation of Powers," *Monthly Review* 66/3 (July–August 2014): 136–59. Bill Moyers and Michael Winship, "Donald Trump's Mission Creep Just Took a Giant Leap Forward," BillMoyers.com, February 1, 2017.
72. Bob Bryan, "Trump Is Officially Making an Economic Promise that Will Be Almost Impossible to Keep," Business Insider, January 22, 2017, http://www.businessinsider.com/trump-4-gdp-growth-promise-2017-1.
73. For a particularly sensitive sociological account of the interests and views underlying Trump's appeal to many white working-class voters, see Arlie Russell Hochschild, *Strangers in Their Own Land* (New York: New Press, 2016), 221–30.
74. Michelle Celarier, "Meet the Wall Street Titans Who Back Trump," *New York*, June 22, 2016; Ben White and Mary Lee, "Trump's 'Big Fat Bubble' Trouble in the Stock Market," Politico, February 24, 2017, http://www.politico.com/story/2017/02/trump-stock-market-bubble-235328.
75. Edward Luce, "Donald Trump Is Creating a Field Day for the 1%," the *Financial Times*, February 26, 2017.
76. Steven Mufson, "Economists Pan Infrastructure Plan Championed by Trump Nominees," *Washington Post*, January 17, 2017; Wilbur Ross and Peter Navarro, "Trump Versus Clinton on Infrastructure," October 27, 2016, http://peternavarro.com/

sitebuildercontent/sitebuilderfiles/infrastructurereport.pdf; Donald Trump, "Remarks by President Trump in Joint Address to Congress," February 28, 2017.

77. Alan Rappeport, "Steven Mnuchin, Treasury Nominee, Failed to Disclose $100 Million in Assets," *New York Times*, January 19, 2017; Dan Kopf, "Trump's First 17 Cabinet Picks Have More Money than a Third of All Americans," Quartz, December 15, 2016, https://qz.com/862412/trumps-16-cabinet-level-picks-have-more-money-than-a-third-of-american-households-combined/; David Smith, "Trump's Billionaire Cabinet Could Be the Wealthiest Administration Ever," *Guardian*, December 2, 2016; Jeremy Scahill, "Notorious Mercenary Erik Prince Advising Trump from the Shadows," The Intercept, January 17, 2017, http://theintercept.com.
78. John Bellamy Foster and Robert W. McChesney, *The Endless Crisis* (New York: Monthly Review Press, 2012), 1.
79. "Whatever Happened to Secular Stagnation?" the *Financial Times*, February 26, 2017. On the deeper causes of secular stagnation, see Harry Magdoff and Paul M. Sweezy, *Stagnation and the Financial Explosion* (New York: Monthly Review Press, 1987).
80. Center for Budget Priorities, "Chart Book: The Legacy of the Great Recession," February 10, 2017; "U.S. Economy Set to Grow Less than 3% for the Tenth Straight Year," Market Watch, December 22, 2015, http://marketwatch.com.
81. Michael W. L. Elsby, Bart Hobijn, and Aysegul Sahin, "The Decline of the U.S. Labor Share," Federal Reserve Bank of San Francisco Working Paper 2013-27, September 2013; Fred Magdoff and John Bellamy Foster, "The Plight of the U.S. Working Class," *Monthly Review* 65/8 (January 2014): 1–22.
82. Timothy Taylor, "Declining U.S. Investment, Gross and Net," ConversableEconomist.blogspot, February 17, 2017.
83. R. Jamil Jonna and John Bellamy Foster, "Marx's Theory of Working-Class Precariousness: Its Relevance Today," *Monthly Review* 67/11 (April 2016): 1–19.
84. "U.S. Household Debts Climbed in 2016 by Most in a Decade," *Wall Street Journal*, February 16, 2017; Andrew Haughwout, Richard Peach, and Joseph Tracy, "A Close Look at the Decline of Homeownership," Federal Reserve Bank of New York, Liberty Street Economics, February 17, 2017, http://libertystreeteconomics.newyorkfed.org.

85. Ben Chu, "The Chart that Shows the UK Is No Longer the Fastest Growing G7 Economy," *Independent*, February 23, 2017; "European Union GDP Annual Growth Rate," Trading Economies, http://tradingeconomies.com; Bureau of Economic Analysis, "GDP and Major NIPA Series, 1929–2012," Survey of Current Business (August 2012): 188 (Table 2a).
86. Foster and McChesney, *The Endless Crisis*, 128.
87. John Bellamy Foster, "The New Imperialism of Globalized Monopoly-Finance Capital," *Monthly Review* 67/3 (July–August 2015): 11–20.
88. Paul Buchheit, "These 6 Men Have as Much Wealth as Half the World's Population," Ecowatch, February 20, 2017, https://www.ecowatch.com/richest-men-in-the-world-2274065153.html. In less than a year, the number decreased from eight to six men, according to a study of 2016 data by Oxfam, "Just 8 Men Own Same Wealth as Half the World," January 16, 2017, https://www.oxfam.org/en/pressroom/pressreleases/2017-01-16/just-8-men-own-same-wealth-half-world. Also see Michael Yates, "Measuring Global Inequality," *Monthly Review* 68/6 (November 2016): 3–4.
89. Mike Patton, "China's Economy Will Overtake the U.S. in 2018," *Forbes*, April 29, 2016.
90. Many of those who see themselves as part of the lower-middle class arguably belong to the working class, as defined by most objective metrics. Strict lines of demarcation are therefore difficult to define. For an objective look at the size the U.S. working class, see R. Jamil Jonna and John Bellamy Foster, "Beyond the Degradation of Labor," *Monthly Review* 66/5 (October 2014): 1–23.
91. For a Marxist perspective on immigration and the U.S. working class, see David L. Wilson, "Marx on Immigration: Workers, Wages, and Legal Status," *Monthly Review* 68/9 (February 2017): 20–28.
92. Samir Amin, "Seize the Crisis!," *Monthly Review* 61/7 (December 2009): 3.
93. Amin, "The Return of Fascism," 3; Amin, "The Surplus in Monopoly Capitalism and the Imperialist Rent,' *Monthly Review* 64/3 (July-August 2012): 78–85.
94. John Bellamy Foster, "The New Geopolitics of Empire," *Monthly Review* 57/8 (January 2006): 1–18.
95. General Wesley K. Clark, *Don't Wait for the Next War* (New York: Public Affairs, 2014), 37–40; John Bellamy Foster, *Naked Imperialism* (New York: Monthly Review Press, 2006).

96. U.S. Defense Intelligence Agency Report on Iraq, 2012, declassified 2015, available at http://judicialwatch.org; Pepe Escobar, "The U.S. Road Map to Balkanize Syria," RT, September 22, 2016, https://www.rt.com/op-edge/360225-us-road-map-balkanize-syria/; Samir Amin, *Russia and the Long Transition from Capitalism to Socialism* (New York: Monthly Review Press, 2016), 104, 127–28; Amin, *The Reawakening of the Arab World* (New York; Monthly Review Press, 2016), 14, 79; Diana Johnstone, *Queen of Chaos* (Petrolia, CA: Counterpunch, 2015).
97. Richard Haass, *A World in Disarray* (New York: Penguin, 2017).
98. Samuel P. Huntington, *The Clash of Civilizations* (New York: Simon and Schuster, 2011).
99. See Gareth Porter, "How the 'New Cold Warriors' Cornered Trump," Consortium News, February 25, 2017, http://consortiumnews.com.
100. Emily Stephenson and Steve Holland, "Trump Vows Military Build-Up, Hammers Nationalist Themes," Reuters, February 25, 2017; Michael D. Shear and Jennifer Steinhauer, "Trump to Seek $54 Billion Increase in Military Spending," *New York Times*, February 27, 2017.
101. Luce, "Donald Trump Is Creating a Field Day for the 1%."
102. Larry Summers, "I'm More Convinced of Secular Stagnation than Ever Before," *Washington Post*, February 17, 2017.
103. Michał Kalecki, *The Last Phase in the Transformation of Capitalism* (New York: Monthly Review Press, 1972), 65–73.
104. The weakening stimulus offered by each dollar of military spending has long been noted. See Baran and Sweezy, *Monopoly Capital*, 213–17.
105. Bertolt Brecht, *Collected Plays*, vol. 6 (New York: Vintage, 1976), 301.
106. See István Mészáros, "The Critique of the State: A Twenty-First Century Perspective," *Monthly Review* 67/4 (September 2015): 23–37; *The Necessity of Social Control*.
107. Donald Trump, "Statement by the President on International Holocaust Remembrance Day," January 27, 2017.
108. Basil Davidson, *Scenes from the Anti-Nazi War* (New York: Monthly Review Press, 1980), 278.

2. This is Not Populism

1. Epigraph: Hitler quoted in Herman Rauschning, *The Voice of De-*

struction (New York: Putnam, 1940), 277.

2. On the analysis of Donald Trump and populism, see, for example, Peter Baker, "As Trump Drifts Away from Populism, His Supporters Grow Watchful," *New York Times*, April 18, 2017; Thomas B. Edsall, "The Peculiar Populism of Donald Trump," *New York Times*, February 2, 2017; Federico Finchelstein and Pablo Piccato, "Donald Trump May Be Showing Us the Future of Right-Wing Politics," *Washington Post*, February 27, 2016; "Why Trump's Populist Appeal Is About Culture Not the Economy," Vox, March 27, 2017, http://vox.com; Perry Anderson, "Passing the Baton," *New Left Review* 103 (2017), 54–55; Leo Panitch, "The Trump Way," *Jacobin* 24 (Winter 2017): 17.
3. The term "populism" has been applied to such varied figures as Adolf Hitler, Charles de Gaulle, Franklin Delano Roosevelt, Mao Zedong, Vladimir Putin, Hugo Chávez, Marine Le Pen, Bernie Sanders, and Donald Trump. See Margaret Canovan, *Populism* (New York: Harcourt Brace Jovanovich, 1981), 292; Jan-Werner Müller, *What Is Populism?* (Philadelphia: University of Pennsylvania Press, 2016), 1, 9, 13, 34–37, 48, 93; Cas Muddle and Cristóbal Kaltwasser, *Populism: A Very Short Introduction* (Oxford: Oxford University Press, 2017), 9, 12–13, 24, 53, 109; Ruth Wodak, *The Politics of Fear* (London: Sage, 2015), 10; "Donald Trump, Xi Jinping and the Mao Factor," CNN, April 3, 2017; David Greenberg, "The Populism of the Roosevelt Era," *Time*, June 24, 2009.
4. Lawrence Goodwyn, *The Populist Moment: A Short History of the Agrarian Revolt in America* (Oxford: Oxford University Press, 1978). In Russia in the late nineteenth century there was a quite different revolutionary populism, which also was tied to agrarian roots. See Franco Venturi, *Roots of Revolution* (New York: Grosset and Dunlap, 1966).
5. Walter Laqueur, *Fascism: Past, Present and Future* (Oxford: Oxford University Press, 1996), 4–8.
6. See Simon Hedlin, "On Trump's Populism, Learn from Sweden's Mistakes," *Forbes*, December 22, 2016; Ruth Wodak, Majid Khosravinik, and Brigitte Mral, eds., *Right-Wing Populism in Europe* (London: Bloomsbury, 2013). On local successes of France's National Front, see Valérie Igounet and Vincent Jarousseau, "Scenes from the Front," *Dissent*, Spring 2017: 88–95.
7. Bertolt Brecht, *Galileo* (New York: Grove Weidenfeld, 1966), 137–38.

8. Charles Bremer, "At the Gates of Power," *New Statesman*, December 4, 2014.
9. Finchelstein and Piccato, "Donald Trump May Be Showing Us the Future of Right-Wing Politics"; Dylan Matthews, "I Asked 5 Fascism Experts Whether Donald Trump Is a Fascist," Vox, December 10, 2015, http://vox.com; Edsall, "The Peculiar Populism of Donald Trump"; "Why Trump's Populist Appeal Is About Culture, Not the Economy"; Sheri Berman, "Populism Is Not Fascism: But it Could Be a Harbinger," *Foreign Affairs*, November-December 2016.
10. Paul A. Baran and Paul M. Sweezy, *Monopoly Capital* (New York: Monthly Review Press, 1966), 155.
11. Slavoj Žižek, *Did Somebody Say Totalitarianism?* (London: Verso, 2001), 2–3. See also Hannah Arendt, *The Origins of Totalitarianism* (New York: Harcourt Brace, 1951), 301–18.
12. On the way that this is connected to Arendt's own views see "Populism Through the Eyes of Hannah Arendt: Now and Then," Eyes on Europe, April 2017, http://eyes-on-europe.eu/populism-through-the-eyes-of-hannah-arendt-now-and-then/. A similar argument on the liberal-democratic designation of a totalitarian-populist nexus to the one that I have presented here, though not discussing Arendt, and tracing the shift in the way the concept of populism was used in the Cold War "vital center" views of thinkers such as Arthur Schlesinger Jr. and Richard Hofstadter, can be found in Marco D'Eramo, "Populism and the New Oligarchy," *New Left Review* 82 (2013): 5–28.
13. Müller, *What Is Populism?*, 2–3, 13, 93, 99–103; Muddle and Kaltwasser, *Populism*, 1–7, 92–96, 108–9, 116–18.
14. On substantive democracy, see István Mészáros, "The Critique of the State: A Twenty-First Century Perspective," *Monthly Review* 67/4 (September 2015): 32–37. On the critique of liberal democracy as a contradictory state form under capitalism see C. B. Macpherson, *The Life and Times of Liberal Democracy* (Oxford: Oxford University Press, 1977).
15. Andrea Mammone, *Transnational Neo-Fascism in France and Italy* (Cambridge: Cambridge University Press, 2015), 7, 16; Laqueur, *Fascism*, 4–8.
16. Laqueur, *Fascism*, 4–9.
17. The term "neo-fascist wind" comes from Mammone, *Transnational Neo-Fascism*. See also Judith Butler, "Trump, Fascism,

and the Construction of 'the People,'" Verso blog, December 29, 2016, http://versobooks.com; Noam Chomsky, "Trump Might Be a Disaster, But His Team Is Ready to Loot America," Alternet, April 15, 2017, http://alternet.org; *Optimism Over Despair* (Chicago: Haymarket, 2017), 113–15; Juan Cole, "Preparing for the Normalization of a Neo-Fascist White House," Informed Comment blog, January 2, 2017, http://juancole.com; Henry A. Giroux, "Combatting Trump's Neo-Fascism and the Ghost of *1984*," Truthout, February 7, 2017, http://truth-out.org; Paul Street, "Slandering Populism," Counterpunch, April 28, 2017, http://counterpunch.org; Cornel West, "Goodbye, American Neoliberalism," *Guardian*, November 7, 2016; Walter Dean Burnham, "Breitbart, Steve Bannon and Donald Trump," London School of Economics, American Politics and Policy blog, October 31, 2016, http://bit.ly/2eM0FnV.

18. Dennis Gilbert, *The American Class Structure in an Age of Growing Inequality* (Los Angeles: Sage, 2011), 14, 243–47. The divisions between the working class and the lower-middle class cannot be determined with precision. As Karl Marx observed, "Middle and transitional levels always conceal the boundaries." Karl Marx, *Capital*, vol. 3 (London: Penguin, 1981), 1025. It is also true that both economic and cultural factors (and consciousness) are part of the determination of class relations in real-historical terms.
19. See pp. 19–21 in Chapter One, above.
20. C. Wright Mills, *White Collar* (Oxford: Oxford University Press, 1951), 353–54. The concept of "crony capitalists" is seen by Bannon as integral to lower-middle-class radicalism. See Bannon quote in Lester Feeder, "This Is How Steve Bannon Sees the Entire World," Buzzfeed, November 15, 2016, https://www.buzzfeed.com/lesterfeder/this-is-how-steve-bannon-sees-the-entire-world?utm_term=.ibkjO8am7#.lg7m1VawO.
21. Roger Griffin, "General Introduction," in *Fascism*, ed. Roger Griffin (Oxford: Oxford University Press, 1995), 3–4.
22. Canovan, *Populism*, 292; Wodak, *The Politics of Fear*, 10; "Pope Francis Warns Against Rise of Populist Leaders 'Like Hitler' as Donald Trump Sworn in as President," *The Independent*, January 22, 2017.
23. Arthur Schweitzer, *Big Business in the Third Reich* (Bloomington: Indiana University Press, 1964): 239–96; Franz Neumann, *Behemoth* (Oxford: Oxford University Press, 1942). The extent to

which notions of organized, corporatist, and state capitalism can be applied to Nazi Germany (prior to 1939) are of course open to dispute. As Franz Neumann argued in *Behemoth*, the Third Reich increased the power of cartels, and the increased organization in the economy seemingly achieved was less through the state than through the heightened dominance of monopoly capital.

24. Karl Bracher, *The German Dictatorship* (New York: Praeger, 1970), 192–93.
25. Bracher, *The German Dictatorship*, 193–98. On the Reichstag fire, see John Mage and Michael E. Tigar, "The Reichstag Fire Trial, 1933–2008," *Monthly Review* 60/10 (March 2009): 24–49.
26. Nikolaus Wachsmann, *Hitler's Prisons* (New Haven: Yale University Press, 2004), 69, 71.
27. Schmitt quoted in Karl Dietrich Bracher, "Stages of Totalitarian Integration (Gleichschaltung)," in *Republic to Reich*, ed. Hajo Holborn (New York: Vintage, 1972), 126.
28. Julius Evola, *Fascism Viewed from the Right* (London: Arktos, 2013), 51; H. T. Hansen, Introduction in Julius Evola, *Men Among the Ruins* (Rochester, VT: Inner Traditions, 2002), 47–48.
29. Maxine Y. Sweezy (see also under Maxine Y. Woolston), *The Structure of the Nazi Economy* (Cambridge, MA: Harvard University Press, 1941), 27–35; Gustav Stolper, *German Economy, 1870–1940* (New York: Reynal and Hitchcock, 1940), 207; Germà Bel, "The Coining of 'Privatization' and Germany's National Socialist Party," *Journal of Economic Perspectives* 20/3 (2006): 187–94; Daniel Guerin, *Fascism and Big Business* (New York: Pathfinder, 1973).
30. Schweitzer, *Big Business in the Third Reich*, 269–78, 327–28.
31. Hitler quoted in Rauschning, *Voice of Destruction*, 91.
32. Sheri Berman, "It Wasn't Just Hate: Fascism Offered Robust Social Welfare," Aeon, March 27, 2017, http://aeon.co; A. James Gregor, *Italian Fascism and Developmental Dictatorship* (Princeton: Princeton University Press, 1979), 256–64; Robert O. Paxton, *The Anatomy of Fascism* (New York: Vintage, 2005), 147.
33. Karl Marx and Frederick Engels famously wrote in *The Communist Manifesto*: "The executive of the modern State is but a committee for managing the common affairs of the whole bourgeoisie." In Marxian theory fascism in the advanced capitalist states is a deviation from this, promoting the interests of monopoly capi-

tal (monopoly-finance capital) primarily, rather than the "whole bourgeoisie." It thus has a narrower foundation and is compatible with a wider repression. See Karl Marx and Frederick Engels, *The Communist Manifesto* (New York: Monthly Review Press, 1964), 5.

34. Enzo Traverso, "Post-Fascism: A Mutation Still Underway," Verso blog, March 13, 2017, http://versobooks.com; Pauline Bock, "The French Millennials Marching Behind Marine Le Pen," *New Statesman*, February 21, 2017; Bremer, "At the Gates of Power"; Kim Wilsher, "Fear of Neo-Fascism Keeps Emmanuel Macron Ahead of Marine Le Pen," *Guardian*, April 29, 2017.
35. See Jayati Ghosh, "Globalization and the End of the Labor Aristocracy," *Dollars and Sense*, March-April 2017.
36. Evola quoted in Paul Furlong, *Social and Political Thought of Julius Evola* (London: Routledge, 2011), 88; Laqueur, *Fascism*, 96; Evola, *Fascism Viewed from the Right*, 55; Hansen, Introduction, in Evola, *Men Among the Ruins*, 48.
37. Ibid., 91–95; Laqueur, *Fascism*, 97; Julius Evola, *The Path of Cinnabar* (London: Integral Tradition, 2009), 88–95. It was Evola's reemergence as a major neo-fascist thinker, coupled with his earlier leading role in the late 1920s in the "Ur-Group" of Italian intellectuals, dedicated to providing pagan bases for right-wing ideology (*Ur* is a prefix standing for primordial), that undoubtedly inspired Umberto Eco's famous 1995 article on "Ur-Fascism," in which Evola was singled out as the chief theoretical figure. "The first feature of Ur-Fascism," Eco wrote, "is the cult of tradition." Umberto Eco, "Ur-Fascism," *New York Review of Books*, June 22, 1995.
38. Evola, *Men Among the Ruins*, 195; H. T. Hansen, Introduction, in Julius Evola, *Revolt Against the Modern World* (Rochester, VT: Inner Traditions, 1995), x; Mammone, *Transnational Neo-Fascism*, 67–68.
39. Julius Evola, *Ride the Tiger* (Rochester, VT: Inner Traditions, 2003), 173.
40. Evola, *Fascism Viewed from the Right*, 101, *Men Among the Ruins*, 75, *Revolt Against the Modern World*, 167–71; Mammone, *Transnational Neo-Fascism*, 70. In the chapter on "The Issue of Race" in his autobiography, *The Path of Cinnabar*, Evola tries to present his racial views as spiritual rather than materialistic and to claim that they were removed from racism; in particular, distinguishing himself from the Nazi race theorist Alfred Rosenberg,

to whom he was frequently compared. However, he contradicts himself by exhibiting racist views on every page even here, not only in his treatments of the "Roman Aryan" race, but also in declaring that "a justification for the Fascist embrace of racism was the well-documented anti-Fascist sentiment of international Jewry." Evola, *The Path of Cinnabar*, 164–67, 173.

41. Evola, *Revolt Against the Modern World*, 169, 355; Evola, *Ride the Tiger*, 131.
42. Evola, *Men Among the Ruins*, 123; Furlong, *The Social and Political Thought of Julius Evola*, 143–45.
43. Mammone, *Transnational Neo-Fascism*, 173–74.
44. Aleksandr Dugin, *The Fourth Political Theory* (London: Arktos, 2012), 13, 28–34, 39–46, 88–89, 95–96, 193; Laqueur, *Fascism*, 195–96; Aleksandr Dugin, "Heidegger and Evola," Middle East Media Research Institute, February 16, 2017. Significantly, Dugin relies particularly on the Nazi phase of Heidegger's work.
45. Jane Mayer, "The Reclusive Hedge-Fund Tycoon Behind the Trump Presidency," *The New Yorker*, March 27, 2017.
46. Dan Schnur, "Trump, the Centrist President," *New York Times*, March 31, 2017; "Slavoj Žižek: 'Trump Is Really a Centrist Liberal,'" *Guardian*, April 28, 2016; Neal Gabler, "Forget Fascism. It's Anarchy We Have to Worry About," *Moyers and Company*, March 29, 2017, http://billmoyers.com.
47. See "All the President's Billionaires," *Forbes*, December 9, 2016. Bannon's notion of "deconstruction of the administrative state," although of no immediate practical impact, seems to have a kind of homologous relation to Dugin's "deconstruction of civilization." See Dugin, *The Fourth Political Theory*, 106–8.
48. "Ralph Nader Denounces Trump Budget as Corporatist, Militarist, and Racist," *Democracy Now!*, March 17, 2017; Ashley Parker and Philip Rucker, "Trump Taps Kushner to Lead a SWAT Team to Fix Government with Business Ideas," *Washington Post*, March 26, 2017.
49. Michael Wolff, "Ringside with Steve Bannon at Trump Tower as the President-Elect's Strategist Plots 'An Entirely New Political Movement,'" *Hollywood Reporter*, November 18, 2016, http://www.hollywoodreporter.com/news/steve-bannon-trump-tower-interview-trumps-strategist-plots-new-political-movement-948747.
50. "CNN Host: 'Donald Trump Became President,' Last Night," The

Hill, April 17, 2017, http://thehill.com; Alex Shephard, "What Just Happened? A Review of President Trump's Twelfth Week," *The New Republic*, April 14, 2017; Zeeshan Aleem, "U.S. Airstrikes Are Killing a Lot More Civilians. And No One Is Sure Why," Vox, March 28, 2017, http://vox.com; Jason Le Miere, "Under Trump U.S. Military Has Allegedly Killed Over 1,000 Civilians in Iraq, Syria in March," *Newsweek*, March 31, 2017.

51. Samuel P. Huntington, *The Clash of Civilizations* (New York: Simon and Schuster, 2011). Trump's original Deputy National Security Advisor, Kissinger's protégé K. T. McFarland, was associated with the shift toward détente with Russia and a harder line on China, widely seen as a strategy pushed by Kissinger himself. Trump's removal of McFarland in April 2017 more than anything else pointed to the end of this geopolitical strategy within the administration. In its place was a more traditional policy of simultaneously pursuing a new Cold War with Russia with a general attempt to expand U.S. power globally.
52. Jeremy W. Peters, "Bannon's Views Can Be Traced to a Book that Warns, 'Winter is Coming,'" *New York Times*, April 8, 2017; Kristin Iversen, "Why It Matters that Hillary Clinton Supports Syria Decision," *Nylon*, April 7, 2017, https://www.nylon.com/articles/hillary-clinton-supports-bombing-syria; William Strauss and Neil Howe, *The Fourth Turning* (New York: Broadway, 1997), 138.
53. The upper-middle-class professional strata increasingly became the focus of the political strategy of Bill and Hillary Clinton. See Thomas Frank, *Listen, Liberal* (New York: Henry Holt, 2016).
54. The notion that fascism gives "expression" to lower-middle-class and working-class demands but does not advance their needs in substance, since aimed principally at promoting capitalism, was introduced in Walter Benjamin, *The Work of Art in the Age of Mechanical Reproduction* (Lexington, KY: Prism, 2010), 47.
55. Breitbart, "An Establishment Conservative's Guide to the Alt-Right," March 29, 2016; Robert Beiner, "The Political Thought of Stephen K. Bannon," Crooked Timber, January 11, 2017, http://crookedtimber.org.
56. Steve Bannon, remarks via Skype at the Human Dignity Conference, the Vatican, summer 2014, transcribed in J. Feeder, "This Is How Steve Bannon Sees the Entire World," Buzzfeed, November

15, 2016; Nina Burleigh, "The Bannon Canon: Books Favored by the Trump Adviser," *Newsweek*, March 23, 2017.

57. Wolff, "Ringside with Steve Bannon at Trump Tower.'"
58. Jean Raspail, *The Camp of the Saints* (New York: Scribner, 1973); Jonathan Ofir, "Steve Bannon's Judeo-Christian 'Camp of the Saints,'" Mondoweiss, March 11, 2017, http://mondoweiss.org; "Racist Book, Camp of the Saints, Gains in Popularity," Southern Poverty Law Center, March 21, 2001.
59. Ofir, "Steve Bannon's Judeo-Christian 'Camp of the Saints.'"
60. Paul Blumenthal, "No Matter What Happens to Bannon, Jeff Sessions Will Press His Anti-Immigrant Agenda," Huffington Post, http://www.huffingtonpost.com/entry/jeff-sessions-steve-bannon_us_58efb376e4b0bb9638e23542 April 13, 2017.
61. Osita Nwanevu, "GOP Congressman Steve King Is Now Endorsing Explicitly Racist Books, Because He's Steve King," Slate, March 14, 2017, GOP Congressman Steve King Is Now Endorsing Explicitly Racist Books, Because He's Steve King. On Bannon's wider, active promotion of barbaric-neo-fascist sensibilities via film see Adam Wren, "What I Learned Binge-Watching Steve Bannon's Documentaries," Politico, December 2, 2016, http://www.politico.com/magazine/story/2016/12/steve-bannon-films-movies-documentaries-trump-hollywood-214495.
62. Breitbart, "Steve Bannon Speaks to Breitbart: The Forgotten Men and Women Who Are the Backbone of this Country Have Risen Up," November 9, 2016; Breitbart, "Steve Bannon: 'Hobbits and Deplorables Had a Great Run in 2016,' But It's Only 'Top of the First Inning,'" December 30, 2016; CNN, "McCain Refers to 'Tea Party Hobbits,' Blasts Bachmann-Backed Idea," July 27, 2011.
63. Baker, "As Trump Drifts Away from Populism, His Supporters Grow Watchful"; Jamelle Bouie, "Trump Sees Himself in Andrew Jackson," Slate, March 15, 2017, http://www.slate.com/articles/news_and_politics/politics/2017/03/donald_trump_sees_himself_in_andrew_jackson_they_deserve_one_another.html; Jonathan Capehart, "Trump's Woefully Ignorant Beliefs about the Civil War and Andrew Jackson," *Washington Post*, Post-Partisan blog, May 1, 2017, https://www.washingtonpost.com/blogs/post-partisan/wp/2017/05/01/trumps-woefully-ignorant-beliefs-about-the-civil-war-and-andrew-jackson/?utm_term=.95dd2a56b6c6.
64. Clip from Donald Trump speech on *CBS Weekend News*, May

7, 2016. Thomas Frank calls the Trump movement "the greatest fake-populist rising the country has ever seen." Frank, *Listen, Liberal*, 261.

65. Donald J. Trump, *Time to Get Tough: Make America Great Again* (Washington, D.C.: Regnery, 2011), 188; Sarah Jaffe, "So Much for 'Draining the Swamp': Wall Street's Power Soars Under Trump," Truthout, April 21, 2017, http://www.truth-out.org/opinion/item/40300-so-much-for-draining-the-swamp-wall-street-s-power-soars-under-trump. On Trump's personality, views, and ambitions see Jane Mayer, "Donald Trump's Ghost Writer Tells All," *The New Yorker*, July 25, 2016.
66. Curtis Ellis, "The Radical Left's Ethnic Cleansing of America," WorldNetDaily, May 20, 2016, http://wnd.com; Breitbart, "Curtis Ellis Discusses 'The Radical Left's Ethnic Cleansing of America,'" May 24, 2016.
67. Cornel West, "Goodbye, American Neoliberalism," *Guardian*, November 7, 2016.
68. Paul M. Sweezy, "More (or Less) on Globalization," *Monthly Review* 49/4 (September 1997): 3.
69. John Bellamy Foster and Robert W. McChesney, *The Endless Crisis* (New York: Monthly Review Press, 2012).
70. Michael D. Yates, *The Great Inequality* (London: Routledge, 2016).
71. Michael Jacobs and Mariana Mazzucato, "Breaking with Capitalist Orthodoxy," *Dissent* (Spring 2017): 36–37.
72. "Nine Charts about Wealth Inequality in America," Urban Institute, http://apps.urban.org.
73. The notion that a small portion of the surplus siphoned from the hegemonic power ended up going to a "small, privileged, 'protected' minority" of workers, stabilizing the system, was first introduced by Engels in the preface to the 1892 English edition of his book, and later taken up by Lenin. See Frederick Engels, *The Condition of the Working Class in England* (Oxford: Oxford University Press, 1993), 323–24; V. I. Lenin, *Imperialism* (New York: International Publishers, 1969).
74. Ghosh, "Globalization and the End of the Labor Aristocracy."
75. CNN, "Exit Polls, Election 2016," November 23, 2016.
76. Peters, "Bannon's Views Can Be Traced to a Book that Warns, 'Winter Is Coming'"; Wolff, "Ringside with Steve Bannon at Trump Tower.'"

77. President Donald Trump, "Inaugural Address," January 21, 2017, http://whitehouse.gov; Trump, *Time to Get Tough*, 9–27; NPR, "Ahead of Trump's First Job Report, a Look at His Remarks on the Numbers," January 29, 2017. The term "truthful hyperbole" was introduced by Trump's ghostwriter in his book *The Art of the Deal*. See Mayer, "Donald Trump's Ghost Writer Tells All."
78. CBS News, "Donald Trump: Black Lives Matter Calls for Killing Police," July 19, 2016.
79. Trump, *Time to Get Tough*, 29–48; Peter Navarro, *The Coming China Wars* (New York: Free Press, 2008), 203–5; Jacob Heilbrun, "The Most Dangerous Man in Trump World?," Politico, February 12, 2017, http://www.politico.com/magazine/story/2017/02/peter-navarro-trump-trade-china-214772.
80. See James K. Galbraith, "Can Trump Deliver on Growth?" *Dissent* (Spring 2017): 43–50; Foster, "Neo-Fascism in the White .House," 19–25.
81. CNN, "Steve Bannon in 2013: Joseph McCarthy Was Right in Crusade against Communist Infiltration," March 6, 2017.
82. Brecht, *Galileo*, 133.
83. Oxford Dictionaries, "The Word of the Year 2016 Is…," November 8, 2016, http://en.oxforddictionaries.com.
84. Georg Lukács, *The Destruction of Reason* (London: Merlin, 1980).
85. Ellen Meiksins Wood, *The Retreat from Class* (London: Verso, 1999).

3. Trump and Climate Catastrophe

1. Epigraph: Donald J. Trump, Twitter post, January 1, 2014, 5:39 p.m., http://twitter.com/realDonaldTrump.
2. Leo Benedictus, "Noam Chomsky on Donald Trump: 'Almost a Death Knell for the Human Species,'" *Guardian*, May 20, 2016; statements by Michael E. Mann quoted in "US Election: Climate Scientists React to Donald Trump's Victory," CarbonBrief, November 9, 2016, http://carbonbrief.org. Mann, in his statement, is also quoting James Hansen, who several years earlier had used the phrase "game over for the climate" in calling for immediate action to address climate change. See James Hansen, "Game Over for the Climate," *New York Times*, May 12, 2012.
3. Shaun Marcott, quoted in "Climate Scientists React to Donald Trump's Victory."

4. James Hansen, *Storms of My Grandchildren* (New York: Bloomsbury, 2009), 269; Kevin Anderson, "Climate Change Going Beyond Dangerous—Brutal Numbers and Tenuous Hope," What Next Forum, September 12, http://whatnext.org; Heidi Cullen, *The Weather of the Future* (New York: HarperCollins, 2011), 261–71.
5. Scott Waldman, "Rise in Global Carbon Emissions Slows," *Scientific American*, November 14, 2016.
6. See James Hansen, "China and the Barbarians: Part I," November 24, 2010, http://columbia.edu; Michael E. Mann and Tom Toles, *The Madhouse Effect* (New York: Columbia University Press, 2016), 139–40; Jean Chemnick, "China Takes the Climate Spotlight as U.S. Heads for Exit," *Scientific American*, November 18, 2016; Naomi Oreskes and Erik M. Conway, *The Collapse of Western Civilization* (New York: Columbia University Press, 2014).
7. World Meteorological Organization, "The Global Climate 2011–2015: Heat Records and High Impact Weather," November 8, 2016, http://public.wmo.int; "Provisional WMO Statement on the Status of the Global Climate in 2016," November 14, 2016, http://public.wmo.int.
8. National Oceanic and Atmospheric Administration (NOAA), "Executive Summary," *Arctic Report Card* (Washington, D.C.: NOAA, 2016), http://arctic.noaa.gov; Henry Fountain and John Schwartz, "Spiking Temperatures in the Arctic Startle Scientists," *New York Times*, December 13, 2016.
9. Brady Dennis and Chris Mooney, "Scientists Nearly Double Sea Level Rise Projections for 2100, because of Antarctica," *Washington Post*, March 30, 2016 (updated December 17, 2016); Michael Oppenheimer and Richard B. Alley, "How High Will the Seas Rise?" *Science* 354/6318 (2016): 1375–76; Julia Rosen, "Sea Level Rise Accelerating Faster than Thought," *Science* news blog, http://sciencemag.org; May 11, 2015; Robert M. DeConto and David Pollard, "Contribution of Antarctic to Past and Future Sea-Level Rise," *Nature* 531 (2016): 591–97; Jeff Tollefson, "Antarctic Model Raises Prospect of Unstoppable Ice Collapse," *Nature*, March 30, 2016, http://nature.com; Brian Kahn, "Sea Level Could Rise at Least 6 Meters," *Scientific American*, July 9, 2015.
10. Kevin Anderson, "Avoiding Dangerous Climate Change Demands De-Growth Strategies from Wealthier Nations," November 25, 2013, http://kevinanderson.info/blog; PBL Netherlands,

Environmental Assessment Agency, Trends in Global CO_2 Emissions, 2016 Report (The Hague: PBL, 2016), 13 http://www.pbl.nl/en. The Netherlands Environmental Agency statistics include carbon from both fossil fuels and cement manufacture.

Hansen further calculates that in order to reduce carbon emissions by 80 percent by 2050, as current models minimally require, it would necessitate an approximately 5 percent annual decline in emissions (on an exponential, or constant percentage rate basis). If a 6 percent annual reduction were to be achieved beginning in 2020, the world could get back down to the necessary 350 ppm of carbon in the atmosphere, that is, if it were additionally to suck 150 gigatonnes of carbon from the atmosphere by means of improved forestry and agricultural practices. The rich, high per-capita emissions countries are those most able to achieve steep initial reductions in carbon emissions, because it is there that the "low-hanging fruit" are primarily to be found. James Hansen, "Rolling Stones," January 11, 2017, http://columbia.edu.

11. Mann and Toles, *The Madhouse Effect*, 28, 132.
12. Ibid., 10–11, 150; Ian Angus, *Facing the Anthropocene* (New York: Monthly Review Press, 2016).
13. The severity of the Anthropocene crisis prompted some major environmental thinkers to shift from mainstream to more radical views critical of capitalism. See, for example, James Gustave Speth, *The Bridge at the Edge of the Time* (New Haven: Yale University Press, 2008).
14. See Paul M. Sweezy and Harry Magdoff, "Capitalism and the Environment," *Monthly Review* 41/2 (June 1989): 1–10; John Bellamy Foster, Brett Clark, and Richard York, *The Ecological Rift* (New York: Monthly Review Press, 2010); Christopher Wright and Daniel Nyberg, *Climate Change, Capitalism, and Corporations* (Cambridge: Cambridge University Press, 2015).
15. The sociologist Max Weber was perhaps the first major thinker to argue that historical capitalism was inextricably intertwined with the fossil-fuel regime. See John Bellamy Foster and Hannah Holleman, "Weber and the Environment," *American Journal of Sociology* 117/6 (2012): 1646–60.
16. For analyses of these global trends of monopoly, finance, stagnation, and imperialism, see Samir Amin, *The Implosion of Contemporary Capitalism* (New York: Monthly Review Press, 2013);

John Bellamy Foster and Robert W. McChesney, *The Endless Crisis* (New York: Monthly Review Press, 2012); Costas Lapavitsas, *Profiting Without Producing* (London: Verso, 2014); Utsa Patnaik and Prabhat Patnaik, *A Theory of Imperialism* (New York: Columbia University Press, 2017); and John Smith, *Imperialism in the Twenty-First Century* (New York: Monthly Review Press, 2016). The shift to financial-wealth accumulation over production and income generation is also captured, from a non-Marxian viewpoint, in Thomas Piketty, *Capital in the Twenty-First Century* (Cambridge, MA: Harvard University Press, 2013).

17. See Foster and McChesney, *The Endless Crisis*, 44–45, 125–54; Amin, *The Implosion of Contemporary Capitalism*.
18. Paul M. Sweezy, *The Theory of Capitalist Development* (New York: Oxford University Press, 1942), 348–52; Sweezy, "Capitalism and the Environment," 8–9.
19. The alt-right, riding high since Trump's election, has been defined by *National Review* as a movement of "white nationalists and wanna-be fascists." Unfortunately, the "wanna-be" seems less and less warranted. David French, "The Race-Obsessed Left Has Released a Monster It Can't Control," *National Review*, January 26, 2016. French tries to blame the rise of the alt-right and Trump on the left, rather than on the right's own "white identity politics."
20. Naomi Klein, *This Changes Everything: Capitalism vs. The Climate* (New York: Simon and Schuster, 2014), 22, 38–39.
21. See Oscar Reyes, "Seven Wrinkles in the Paris Climate Deal," Foreign Policy in Focus, December 14, 2015, http://fpif.org; Kelly Levin and Taryn Fransen, "Why Are INDC Studies Reaching Different Temperature Estimates?" World Resources Institute, November 9, 2015, http://wri.org/blog.
22. U.S. carbon emissions had already fallen by 13 percent between 2005 and 2013, largely due to the shift away from coal during the fracking boom, making Obama's plan even less ambitious than it appeared. See the *2017 Economic Report of the President* (Washingotn, D.C.: U.S. Government Publishing Office), 423–82; Mark Hertsgaard, "Climate Change," *The Nation*, January 2 and 9, 2017, 72; Brad Plumer, "A Guide to Obama's New Rules to Cut Carbon Emissions from Power Plants," Vox.com, June 1, 2014, http://vox.com; David Biello, "How Far Does Obama's Clean Power Plan Go in Slowing Climate Change?," *Scientific American*, August 6, 2015.

23. 2017 Economic Report of the President, 448, 472, 483. On the debate on the left over Obama's CCP and more radical strategies, see Christian Parenti, "Climate Change: What Role for Reform?"; and the Editors, "A Reply to Parenti," *Monthly Review* 65/11 (April 2014): 49–55.
24. Tony Dokoupil, "Obama's Climate Policy Is 'Practically Worthless,' Says Expert," MSNBC, August 4, 2015.
25. This is the thesis advanced in Hans-Werner Sinn, *The Green Paradox* (Cambridge, MA: MIT Press, 2012).
26. Henry Fountain and Erica Goode, "Trump Has Options for Undoing Obama's Climate Legacy," *New York Times*, November 25, 2016; "Trump Will Withdraw U.S. from Paris Climate Agreement," *New York Times*, June 1, 2017.
27. Ewan Palmer, "50 Other Times Donald Trump Denied Climate Change and Global Warming," *International Business Times*, September 27, 2016, http://ibtimes.co.uk.
28. Henry Fountain, "Trump's Climate Contrarian: Myron Ebell Takes on the EPA," *New York Times*, November 11, 2016; Matt Shuham, "Trump Adviser: Global Warming Could Be Disproven Just Like Flat Earth Theory," TalkingPointsMemo, December 14, 2016, http://talkingpointsmemo.com; Mazin Sidahmed, "Climate Change Denial in the Trump Cabinet: Where Do Nominees Stand?" *Guardian*, December 15, 2016; Tim Murphy, "Rick Perry's War on Science," *Mother Jones*, December 13, 2016; Lee Fang, "He Waged Intimidation Campaigns Against Climate Scientists; Now He's Helping Trump Remake the EPA," The Intercept, December 9, 2016, http://theintercept.com; Dan Vergano, "Trump Transition Lawyer Has Spent Years Suing for Climate Emails," Buzzfeed, December 13, 2016, http://buzzfeed.com; Michael E. Mann, *The Hockey Stick and the Climate Wars* (New York: Columbia University Press, 2012), 367–68; Nick Surgey, "Revealed: The Trump Administration's Energy Plan," PR Watch, December 4, 2016, http://prwatch.org; Steven Mufson, "Trump's Energy Policy Team Includes Climate Change Skeptic, Free-Market Advocate," *Washington Post*, November 29, 2016; Scott Pruitt and Luther Strange, "The Climate-Change Gang," *National Review*, May 17, 2016; John Cook, "Yes, There Really Is Scientific Consensus on Climate Change," *Bulletin of the Atomic Scientists*, April 13, 2016, http://thebulletin.org; Charlie Rose, "Charlie Rose Talks to ExxonMobil's Rex Tillerson," Bloomberg TV, March 7, 2013, http://bloomberg.com.

29. Coral Davenport, "Climate Change Conversations Are Targeted in Questionnaire to Energy Department," *New York Times*, December 9, 2016; Chris Mooney and Juliet Eilperin, "Trump Transition Says Request for Names of Climate Scientists Was 'Not Authorized,'" *Washington Post*, December 14, 2016.
30. Matthew Philips, Mark Drajem, and Jennifer A. Dlouhy, "How Climate Rules Might Fade Away," Bloomberg, December 15, 2016; Mufson, "Trump's Energy Policy Team Includes Climate Change Skeptic."
31. James Hansen, "The Real Deal: Usufruct and the Gorilla," DeSmogBlog, August 16, 2007, http://desmogblog.com; Mark Bowen, *Censoring Science* (New York: Penguin, 2008), 303–4.
32. Naomi Oreskes and Erik M. Conway, *Merchants of Doubt* (New York: Bloomsbury, 2011).
33. Thomas Heath, "How a Trump Presidency Will Affect 15 Industries," *Washington Post*, November 12, 2016; Michelle Conlin, "Exclusive: Trump Considering Fracking Mogul Harold Hamm as Energy Secretary," Reuters, July 21, 2016; James Delingpole, "Trump: The Left Just Lost the War on Climate Change," Breitbart, November 9, 2016, http://breitbart.com.
34. Peter Andreas, "Yes, Trump Will Build His Border Wall. Most of It Is Already Built," *Washington Post,* Monkey Cage blog, November 21, 2016; Peter Schwartz and Doug Randall, *An Abrupt Climate Change Scenario and Its Implications for United States National Security* (Pasadena: California Institute of Technology, 2003); John Bellamy Foster, *The Ecological Revolution* (New York: Monthly Review Press, 2009), 107–20.
35. A. B. Spellman, "Interview with Malcolm X," *Monthly Review* 16/1 (May 1964): 23.
36. Eric S. Godoy and Aaron Jaffe, "We Don't Need a 'War' on Climate Change, We Need a Revolution," *New York Times*, October 31, 2016.
37. Fyodor Dostoevsky, *Notes from Underground* (New York: Vintage, 1993), 13; Paul A. Baran, *The Longer View* (New York: Monthly Review Press, 1969), 104. The phrase "vomits up reason" is taken from Baran's interpretation of the Underground Man's rejection of the "laws of nature" and "two times two is four."
38. Klein, *This Changes Everything*, 56, 449; Kevin Anderson, "Why Carbon Prices Can't Deliver the 2°C Target," August 13, 2013, http://kevinanderson.info/blog.

39. Klein, *This Changes Everything*, 7–10, 294.
40. Lauren Regan, "Water Protectors File Class Action Suit for Retaliation and Excessive Force Against Brutal Police," Civil Liberties Defense Center, November 28, 2016, http://cldc.org; "News Timeline of Standing Rock Water Protectors' Resistance to Dakota Access Pipeline," Daily Kos, October 11, 2016, http://dailykos.com; Wes Enzinna, "Crude Awakening," *Mother Jones* (January–February 2017): 32–37; Jack Healy, "As North Dakota Pipeline Is Blocked, Veterans at Standing Rock Cheer," *New York Times*, December 5, 2016.
41. Unconventional fossil fuels are often dirtier, as in the cases of oil sands and oil shale. In other instances, they represent such a great expansion of fossil-fuel availability—as in tight oil and shale gas (via fracking), and ultra-deep oil wells, particularly in the Arctic, now opening up to oil exploration—that they put an end to any expectation of any "peaking" of fossil fuels in time to alleviate the pressure on the climate. Fracking is also associated with methane leaks, which further exacerbate climate change. It should be noted that Hansen himself sees fourth-generation nuclear energy (still not fully developed) as a possible alternative, non-carbon energy source, and thus part of the answer to global warming. This would be a Faustian bargain, however, raising a host of concerns for humanity and the environment.
42. John Bellamy Foster, "James Hansen and the Climate Change Exit Strategy," *Monthly Review* 64/9 (February 2013): 1–18; Foster, "The Fossil Fuels War," *Monthly Review* 65/4 (September 2013): 4–5; Bowen, *Censoring Science*, 305.
43. Anderson, "Why Carbon Prices Can't Deliver."
44. See Fred Magdoff and John Bellamy Foster, *What Every Environmentalist Needs to Know About Capitalism* (New York: Monthly Review Press, 2011), 124–31; Angus, *Facing the Anthropocene*, 189–223.
45. See, for example, the multifaceted threat that capitalism poses toward oceans and marine life, as depicted in Stefano B. Longo, Rebecca Clausen, and Brett Clark, *The Tragedy of the Commodity: Oceans, Fisheries, and Aquaculture* (New Brunswick, NJ: Rutgers University Press, 2015).
46. "If we do not now dare everything, the fulfillment of that prophecy, re-created from the Bible in song by a slave, is upon us: 'God gave Noah the rainbow sign / No more water, the fire

next time.'" James Baldwin, *The Fire Next Time* (New York: Dial, 1963), 105–6.

The Nature of the Resistance: A Brief Conclusion

1. Epigraph: Karl Marx and Frederick Engels, *Collected Works,* vol. 15 (New York: International Publishers, 1975), 485.
2. "We Finally Have Photos of Steve Bannon Whiteboard of Trump Promises," Breitbart, May 3, 2017, http://www.breitbart.com/big-government/2017/05/03/finally-know-steve-bannons-white-board-donald-trump-promises-voters/; "Rabbi Shmuley: For Steve Bannon, Israel is on the Whiteboard," Breitbart, May 3, 2017, http://www.breitbart.com/big-government/2017/05/03/whiteboard-rabbi-shmuley-steve-bannon-israel/; NBC News, "Steve Bannon's Whiteboard To-Do List Exposed on Twitter by Rabbi," May 3, 2017, http://www.nbcnews.com/politics/donald-trump/steven-bannon-s-whiteboard-do-list-exposed-twitter-rabbi-n754291. One promise barely visible on the whiteboard photo was moving the U.S. embassy in Israel to Jerusalem.
3. Breitbart, "We Finally Have Photos of Steve Bannon Whiteboard of Trump Promises." It is now known that Bannon continued to communicate with and influence Breitbart after entering the White House as Trump's chief strategist, for which he has been given a retroactive blank check from the president, in violation of standard rules of ethics in governance. See Matthew Rasza, "A Retroactive Ethics Waiver that Applies to Steve Bannon May Have Broken Ethics Rules," Salon, June 2, 2017, http://www.salon.com/2017/06/02/a-retroactive-ethics-waiver-that-applies-to-steve-bannon-may-have-broken-ethics-rules/.
4. Walter Dean Burnham, *The Current Crisis in American Politics* (Oxford: Oxford University Press, 1983).
5. Walter Dean Burnham, "Political Immunization and Political Confessionalism: The United States and Weimar Germany," *Journal of Interdisciplinary History* 3/1 (Summer 1972): 1–30. For a consideration of the origins of U.S. fascist movements in the 1930s and after see Michael Joseph Roberto, "The Origins of American Fascism," *Monthly Review* 69/2 (June 2017): 26–41.
6. Burnham, "Political Immunization and Political Confessionalism," 29; Walter Dean Burnham, "Breitbart, Steve Bannon and Donald Trump," London School of Economics, American Politics and Policy blog, October 31, 2016, http://bit.ly/2eM0FnV;

Karl Marx and Frederick Engels, *Basic Writings on Politics and Philosophy*, ed. Lewis S. Feuer (Garden City: New York: Doubleday, 1959), 17-18.

7. Burnham, "Political Immunization and Political Confessionalism," 3, 30. On the nature of the bourgeois *Honoriatorenpartei*, or limited-liability parties, relying on local volunteers during electoral contests, while devoid of any definite program, and ruled by permanent leaders and party bureaucrats, see Max Weber, *Economy and Society* (Berkeley: University of California Press, 1978), part 2, 1444–45.
8. Burnham, "Breitbart, Steve Bannon and Donald Trump."
9. Ibid.
10. See "Donald Trump Sexism Tracker: Every Offensive Comment in One Place," *Telegraph*, January 20, 2017, http://www.telegraph.co.uk/women/politics/donald-trump-sexism-tracker-every-offensive-comment-in-one-place/; "Here Are 16 Examples of Donald Trump Being Racist," HuffingtonPost, February 16, 2017, http://www.huffingtonpost.com/entry/president-donald-trump-racist-examples_us_584f2ccae4b0bd9c3dfe5566.
11. Burnham, "Political Immunization and Political Confessionalism," 6; Burnham, "Breitbart, Steve Bannon and Donald Trump."
12. "Hate Groups Increase for Second Consecutive Year as Trump Electrifies Radical Right," Southern Poverty Law Center, February 15, 2017, https://www.splcenter.org/news/2017/02/15/hate-groups-increase-second-consecutive-year-trump-electrifies-radical-right.
13. Michael A. Gould-Wartofsky, *The Occupiers* (Oxford: Oxford University Press, 2015).
14. See Brent Budowsky, "Why Sanders Would Have Defeated Trump in 2016," The Hill, May 5, 2017, http://thehill.com/blogs/pundits-blog/presidential-campaign/332097-why-sanders-would-have-defeated-trump-in-2016; David Horsey, "President Sanders?: Bernie Would Have Beaten Trump," *LA Times,* December 22, 2016, http://www.latimes.com/opinion/topoftheticket/la-na-tt-bernie-beats-trump-20161222-story.html.
15. Conor Lynch, "Yes, Bernie Would Probably Have Won—And His Resurgent Left-Wing Populism Is the Way Forward," Salon, May 5, 2017, http://www.salon.com/2017/05/05/yes-bernie-would-probably-have-won-and-his-resurgent-left-wing-populism-is-the-way-forward/.

16. Although Sanders lost the Democratic Party nomination to Clinton independent of the super-delegate votes, the existence of the latter was continually used to convince his potential supporters that he could not possibly win and thus to discourage their participation.
17. Salim Muwakkil, "The Paradox of Bernie Sanders and the Black Voter," *In These Times*, April 12, 2016, http://inthesetimes.com/article/19020/why-arent-more-black-voters-supporting-bernie-sanders.
18. David Harvey, *The Enigma of Capital* (Oxford: Oxford University Press, 2010), 237.
19. The Movement for Black Lives (M4BL), "Platform," https://policy.m4bl.org/platform/.

Index

Acosta, R. Alexander, 39
African Americans (blacks), 117
Albedo effect, 91
Almirante, Giorgio, 70
Althusser, Louis, 23
Alt-right, 29, 72; in Bannon's ideology, 32; Evola as hero to, 33; "Hobbits" and, 79–80; on sovereignty of U.S., 41; in Trump administration, 77; Trump and, 72
Amin, Samir, 30, 49–50
Anderson, Kevin, 106–7, 109
Anti-imperialism, 118
Arctic region, 90–91
Arendt, Hannah, 59, 60

Bannon, Steve: on administrative state, 36; *Camp of the Saints* and, 78–79; conflicts between media and, 40–41; on foreign policy, 76; global warming denied by, 103–4; on HSC Principals Committee, 35; Islamophobia of, 51; as Kushner's rival, 74; McCarthyism of, 85–86; neo-fascist ideology of, 32–34, 114; removed from National Security Council, 75; as Trump's campaign manager, 72–73, 83–84; as Trump's chief strategist, 77; Trump's Inaugural Address written by, 31, 84; whiteboard of, 111–12
Baran, Paul, 60
Berkeley, University of California at, 39–40
Berman, Sheri, 67–68
Black Lives Matter, 38, 84
Blacks (African Americans), 117
Blockadia, 107
Boteach, Shmuley, 111
Bracher, Karl, 65
Brecht, Bertolt, 24, 53–54, 58, 86, 87

Breitbart News, 111; on Bannon's whiteboard, 112; Burnham on, 114; global warming denied by, 103–4; in Trump campaign, 72
Bulletin of Atomic Scientists, 23
Burnham, Walter Dean, 112–14

The Camp of the Saints (novel, Raspail), 78–79
Capitalism: Bannon on, 32; climate change tied to, 93–96; fascism tied to, 58; socialism as antonym of, 61–62
Carbon emissions, 91–93; failure of reforms on, 96–104; fees for, 108–9
Chile, 11
China: in Bannon's ideology, 32; climate change and, 90; economy of, 46, 48; Navarro on, 84–85; Trump's policies on, 51–52
Chomsky, Noam, 40, 89
Civil liberties, 9
Civil War (U.S.), 80
Clean Power Plan (CPP), 97–100
Climate change, 23; capitalism tied to, 93–96; Ebell on, 36–37; evidence on, 90–93; failure of carbon reforms to control, 96–104; movement on, 107–9; Trump on, 86; Trump administration on, 89–90
Clinton, Hillary: black support for, 117; neoliberalism of, 44; Syria policy of, 51, 76
Crimea, 51

Dakota Access Pipeline, 107
Davidson, Basil, 55
De Benoist, Alain, 71, 72
Democracy: liberal democracy, 59–60; rejected by fascism, 30; totalitarianism versus, 60–61
Democratic Party, Sanders blocked by, 83, 117
DeVos, Betsy, 39, 45
Diego-Rosell, Pablo, 20
Dugin, Aleksandr, 72

Ebell, Myron, 36–37, 99–100
Edsall, Thomas, 59
Education, Trump policies on, 39–40
Education vouchers, 39
Election campaign of 2016, 44; Sanders in, 83, 117–18; Trump's comments in, 15; Trump's promises during, 111; Trump voters in, 20

Ellis, Curtis, 81
Enabling Act (Germany, 1933), 28, 65
Energy Department (U.S.), 101–2
Engels, Frederick, 113
Environmentalism, cutting agencies for, 36–37
Environmental Protection Agency (EPA), 37; Clean Power Plan and, 97, 99; under Trump administration, 100–101
Europe: neo-fascism in, 15, 71–72; right-wing populism, 57–58
European Union, economic growth in, 47
Evola, Julius, 33–34, 66–67; Bannon and, 77; in neo-fascism thought, 69–71; Trump and, 72
Executive branch of federal government, 42
ExxonMobil (firm), 101

Falk, Richard, 23
Fascism, 7–13, 22–26; as antonym of liberal democracy, 61; Brecht on, 53–54; Evola's, 33, 69–71; in Germany, 26–27; as legal revolution, 64; neo-fascism and, 30; populism and, 59; tied to capitalism, 58; vulnerability of U.S. to, 113
Federal government: environmental protection agencies in, 37; Trump's attacks on, 36
Finchelstein, Federico, 59
Flynn, Michael, 35, 52, 75
Fossil fuels, 98–99; pipelines for, 107; price of, 108; stocks in, 103
France, 32
Francis (pope), 37
Friedman, Milton, 11

G7 countries, 47
Geopolitics, 50–52, 75
Germany: fascism in, 26–27, 67–68; *Gleichschaltung* in, 27–29, 65–66
Gingrich, Newt, 36
Gleichschaltung, 27–29, 65–66; Trumpism and, 29–43
Global North, 47–48
Global South, 47–48, 83, 110
Global warming, *see* Climate change
Godoy, Eric S., 105–6
Gorka, Sebastian, 31
Great Recession (2007-2009), 46

Haass, Richard, 51
Hahn, Julia, 32, 42
Hamilton, Richard F., 21

Hamm, Harold, 103
Hansen, H. T., 70
Hansen, James, 89, 98–100, 102–3, 108–9
Hate crimes, 116
Haushofer, Karl, 50
Heidegger, Martin, 28, 72
Herman, Edward, 40
Hertsgaard, Mark, 97
Higher education, 39–40
Hindenburg, Paul von, 28
Hitler, Adolf, 21–22, 26; Evola and, 70; on German legal system, 66; Keynesian economic policies of, 53; on power politics, 57; on state power, 64–65; tax policies of, 67; unilateral power given to, 28, 29
Hobbit Camps, 72, 79–80
Huntington, Samuel, 51

Immigration: Bannon on, 79; climate change and, 104; as issue in election of 2016, 21; Trump's announced policies on, 34; Trump's campaign promises on, 111–12
Income inequality, 48
Independence Party (United Kingdom), 32, 58
Infrastructure, 44–45, 85
Intelligence community, 35
International Holocaust Remembrance Day, 55
Internationalism, 118
Iraq, 51
Islam, 32, 34
Italy, 29, 66–67

Jackson, Andrew, 80
Jacobs, Michael, 82
Jaffe, Aaron, 105–6
Judeo-Christian West, 32–34, 77
Judiciary: expansion of executive power at expense of, 43; in Germany, 66; Trump's attacks on, 34; vacancies in, 35

Kaltwasser, Cristobal, 61
Keynesianism, 53
King, Steve, 79
Klein, Naomi, 96, 106–7
Koch, Charles and David, 12
Kushner, Jared, 75
Kyoto Protocol (1997), 97–98

Labor unions, 38
Laqueur, Walter, 62–63, 69–70
Left-wing populism, 57
Legal systems, 66–67
Le Pen, Marine, 32, 69
Liberal democracy, 24, 25; totalitarianism versus, 60–61

Libertarianism, 8–12
London, Jack, 19
Lukács, Georg, 87

Mackinder, Halford, 50
MacLean, Nancy, 8–9
Malcolm X, 104–5
Mammone, Andrea, 62, 72
Mann, Michael E., 89, 92–93, 100
Marx, Karl, 111, 113
Matthews, Dylan, 59
Mazzucato, Mariana, 82
McCain, John, 79
McCarthy, Joseph, 86
McChesney, Robert W., 46
Media, Trump's conflicts with, 40–41
Mercer, Rebekah, 73
Mercer, Robert, 73
Metabolic rift, 106
Mexico, proposed wall between U.S. and, 73, 84, 104, 112
Military spending: Keynesianism of, 53; Trump's increase in, 52
Miller, Stephen, 31, 84
Mills, C. Wright, 63
Mnuchin, Steven, 45
Movement for Black Lives, 118
Moyers, Bill, 43
Muddle, Cas, 61
Muller, Jan-Werner, 61
Muslims, immigration ban on, 34
Mussolini, Benito, 64, 66; Evola and, 69–70

National Front (France), 32, 58, 69
National Oceanic and Atmospheric Administration (NOAA), 37, 90–91
National Public Radio (NPR), 41
National Review (magazine), 41
National Socialist party (Nazi Party; Germany), *see* Nazi Party
Native Americans, 107
NATO (North Atlantic Treaty Organization), 50–51
Navarro, Peter, 84–85
Nazi Party (National Socialist party; Germany), 21; *Gleichschaltung* policy of, 27–29; populism of, 64
Neo-fascism, 19–20; aim of, 29; attacks on media and, 41; Evola and, 70–71; fascism and, 30; fascism distinguished from, 22–23; as "legal revolution," 68–69; nationalism of, 50; populism and, 58,

59; Trump and, 72–76; Trumpism as, 15, 114–16
Neoliberalism, 7–12, 54, 81–82; of Hillary Clinton, 44
Northern League (Italy), 58

Obama, Barack: on federal detention powers, 42, 43; Trump's attacks on, 114; white supremacist response to, 116
Obama administration, climate policy of, 97–99
Occupy movement, 116

Paris Climate Agreement (2015), 97, 99, 100
Party for Freedom (Netherlands), 58
Paxton, Robert O., 29
Peabody Energy (firm), 103
Pence, Michael, 35
Perry, Rick, 101
Persian Gulf, 50
Piccato, Pablo, 59
Pinochet, Augusto, 11
Pipelines, 107
Popular Front, 54, 109
Populism, 57–64
"Post-truth," 87
Poulantzas, Nicos, 27
Presidency, expansion of powers of, 42–43
Prince, Erik, 45
Prisons, privatization of, 37–38
Privatization: of federal prisons, 37–38; in Nazi Germany, 26–27, 67; of schools, 38, 39; in Trumpism, 29
Pruitt, Scott, 100–101
Public education, 39
Putin, Vladimir, 50–51
Puzder, Andrew, 38
Pyle, Thomas, 100

Racism, 11–12, 37–38, 59
Randall, Doug, 104
Raspail, Jean, 78–79
Reichstag fire (1933), 28, 65
Republican Party: conflicts between media and, 41; neoliberal control over, 12; under Trump, 42
Revolution, 104–5
Right-to-work laws, 38
Right-wing populism, 57–59
Ross, Wilbur, Jr., 45
Rothwell, Jonathan, 20
Ruddy, Chris, 36
Russia, 50–51, 74
Ryan, Paul, 42

Sanders, Bernie, 44; in election campaign of 2016, 83, 117–18
Scaramucci, Anthony, 100
Schmitt, Carl, 27–29, 72

Schnare, David, 100
Schools, privatization of, 38, 39
Schwartz, Peter, 104
Sea levels, 91
Sessions, Jeff, 79, 101
Social cost of carbon (SCC), 102
Socialism, 13; as antonym of capitalism, 61–62; movement towards, 55, 110, 117; Sanders campaign and, 118
South China Sea, 51–52
Soviet Union, 60
Spencer, Richard, 33
Spengler, Oswald, 77
Spykman, Nicholas John, 50
Standing Rock (North Dakota), 107
State: Bannon on, 34, 36; Evola on, 71; power concentrated in, in fascism, 64–65
Stiglitz, Joseph, 31
Stock market, 44
Stone, Roger, 36
Summers, Larry, 53
Supreme Court (U.S.): on Clean Power Plan, 99; on right-to-work laws, 38
Sweden Democrats, 58
Sweezy, Maxine Yaple, 26–27
Sweezy, Paul, 8, 25, 60, 81–82
Syria, 51, 75
System Change Not Climate Change movement, 118

Taxation: in Nazi Germany, 67; Trump's campaign promises on, 112
Thiel, Peter, 73
Tillerson, Rex, 45, 101
Tipping points, 92
Totalitarianism, 60–61
Tough Times: Make America Great Again (Trump), 80
Traditionalist movement, 33, 70
Trans-Pacific Partnership (TPP), 52, 84
Trenberth, Kevin, 99–100
Trump, Donald J.: Burnham on, 114; campaign promises of, 111; on climate change, 89, 99; economic policies of, 43–48, 52–53, 81–86; in election campaign of 2016, 15; foreign policies of, 51–52; Inaugural Address of, 30–31, 84; intelligence community's conflicts with, 35; on International Holocaust Remembrance Day, 55; media's conflicts with, 40–41; Muslim ban announced by, 34; neo-fascist movement and, 72–76; outlook and ambitions

of, 80–81; as post-fascist, 59; Republican Party support for, 12
Trump, Donald J., Jr., 21
Trump administration: agenda of, 73; climate policies of, 89–90, 100–104; competing allegiances within, 76–77; foreign policy of, 76; on oil pipelines, 107; rivalries in, 74
Trumpism, 15; *Gleichschaltung* and, 29–43; neo-fascism of, 114–16
Turning Point USA (organization), 40

Ukraine, 50–51
Unemployment, 47; in Nazi Germany, 68
United Kingdom, 32
United States: Bannon on sovereignty of, 41; carbon-dioxide emissions of, 90, 97–98; decline in hegemony of, 43–53; economic growth in, 47; employees of federal government of, 36; history of populism in, 57; neo-fascism in, 15–16, 71–72; right-wind populism in, 58; vulnerability to fascism of, 113
Universities, under Nazism, 28

Wachsmann, Nikolaus, 65–66
Wallace, George, 112
Wealth inequality, 9, 47, 82
The Weekly Standard (magazine), 41
West, Cornel, 37, 81
White House National Trade Council, 84
Whites, 81; Trump voters among, 20
Winship, Michael, 43
Wolfowitz, Paul, 50
World Meteorological Organization, 90

Yates, Michael, 82
Yiannopoulos, Milo, 39–40

Zakaria, Fareed, 75
Žižek, Slavoj, 60–61
Zinke, Ryan, 101